READY MADE CVs

THE TIMES

4TH EDITION

READY MADE CVs

Winning CVs for EVERY type of job

LYNN WILLIAMS

KOGAN PAGE

First Indian Edition 2009

Kogan Page India Private Limited
4737/23 Ansari Road,
Daryaganj
New Delhi 110 002

This edition is for sale in the Indian subcontinent only. Not for export elsewhere.

ISBN-10: 81-7554-475-9
ISBN-13: 978-81-7554-475-8

Published by Vinod Vasishtha for Kogan Page India Private Limited,
4737/23, Ansari Road, Daryaganj, New Delhi 110 002.

Printed and bound by Raj Press, R-3, Inderpuri, New Delhi - 110 012.

Contents

How to use this book

Even just a few years ago, unless you were either very ambitious or very unlucky you could expect to go to work in an organisation straight from school or college and stay there, gradually moving up the promotion ladder until you retired.

Today, career advancement is more uncertain. Most people will change jobs several times during their working lives; some will even change careers. Increasingly, a good CV is an essential tool in the survival kit of every employee.

What is a good CV, though? The short answer is: one that gets you an interview for the job you want.

Imagine you're the employer for a moment. You have 150 CVs on your desk and from them you have to choose just a handful of applicants to interview. What are you looking for? How do you decide? My bet is that you would pick people who look as though they know how to do the job. People, that is, who:

- have the skills the job requires;
- have experience relevant to the job;
- have successfully handled similar challenges in the past.

As an employer with 150 career histories to read, you would be grateful, too, to the people who made those facts easy to find on their CV.

This book is about making those facts easy to find, and how to highlight them to your best advantage. The first four chapters look in detail at what is in a CV – how to select what goes in and what stays out, layout and presentation, and how to make a good first impression.

Few people, however, have absolutely straightforward careers, and some CVs are trickier to write than others. So Chapters 5 to 8 look at some of the problems that people encounter, and how to handle them. They show how, by highlighting key parts of your CV, you can emphasise your strengths rather than stressing your weaknesses. They also look at CVs for specific 'tricky' situations – getting your first job, returning to work after a career break, continuing in work as a mature employee or after retirement.

The remaining chapters give further examples of CVs. These are written especially for specific categories of jobs – creative positions, sales vacancies, managerial posts, and so on.

Different types of job often emphasise different features when it comes to what makes a person right for that position. Some jobs rely heavily on personal qualities, some demand specific academic qualifications, while others require evidence of achievement in that particular field. These chapters show how, by highlighting and strengthening the relevant parts of your CV, you can emphasise these key points and put them across to a prospective employer effectively.

This book also shows you how to use two special sections of your CV to tailor it specifically for each and every job you apply for so that your suitability for the position stands out so well that an employer would need a really good reason *not* to interview you. Most of the example CVs you will see here have been customised in this way.

If you want to, you can follow the layout of the CV examples in this book to compile your own CV. Each, when typed or printed on to A4 paper, runs to two pages – the recommended length for a CV. Each example puts the key facts and the high-priority information that tells an employer you know how to do the job on the front page, with back-up and lower-priority details on the second page.

Whether you're looking for your first job, aiming for promotion or applying for the job of your dreams, you can put together a CV that shows your future employer your skills and experience clearly and concisely – these examples show you how.

1

The basic CV

A CV, sometimes called a Curriculum Vitae or a résumé, is a summary of your career history, and the skills and experience you have gained during the course of it.

A good CV should:

- attract attention;
- create a good impression;
- present your relevant skills and qualities clearly and concisely.

The aim of a CV

The purpose of a CV is to show a prospective employer that you have the necessary qualities and qualifications to do the job you're applying for. The aim is to get you an interview with that employer, so it needs to demonstrate clearly that you have:

- the specific skills needed for the job;
- the right sort of experience for the job;
- the personal qualities for the position;
- an understanding of the specific requirements of the job.

Keep it simple

The easier a CV is to read, the better. An advertised job vacancy will often attract hundreds of replies, and even the most conscientious employers have very little time to digest every CV that crosses their desk. The best way to make sure that yours gets read is to:

- **Keep it short.** No more than two A4 pages.
- **Keep it clear.** Make it easy to read. A CV should always be printed, and well laid out with wide margins, clear section headings, and the information organised in a logical, easy-to-follow way.
- **Keep it relevant.** The employer usually has two main questions in mind when looking at an employee or potential employee:
  - Is this person able to do the job?
  - Will this person fit in with the rest of us?

Create an impression

As well as keeping your CV short, clear and relevant, make it look businesslike and professional too.

Use:

- plain white or cream A4 size paper;
- good-quality paper – 100 gsm weight;
- a good, clear typeface;
- plain black ink.

Avoid:

- gimmicks;
- sending photocopies;
- spelling and grammar mistakes;
- alterations and amendments – always print off a fresh, correct copy.

The following pages give a template, showing what goes where, followed by a completed CV.

(**Your Name** in large, bold type)
(Your full address)

____

____

____

(Postcode)

(Telephone number, including area code)
(E-mail address)

Career profile

(A brief, businesslike description of yourself)
(Skills)
(Experience)
(Personal strengths)

Key strengths

(Your skills, experience and personal qualities that most closely match the job requirements)

Key skills

- (The main skills you have developed)
- (Particularly those appropriate to the job you are applying for)
-
-
-

Career history

(**Name of company**, usually starting with the most recent)
(Dates you worked there)
(**Job title**)
(Brief description of what you did)

(Brief description of what you achieved in this position)

-
-
-

(**Name of company**)
(Dates you worked there)
(**Job title**)
(Brief description of what you did)

(Brief description of what you achieved in this position)

-
-
-

Name (cont.)

(Name of company)
(Dates you worked there)
(Job title)
(Brief description of what you did. Jobs you did some years ago require less detail than your more recent ones)

Education and training

(Starting with the highest, most recent OR most relevant qualification)

(Name of school, college or university)
(Dates you attended)
(The qualification you achieved)
(You could include brief details of what was covered in the course, especially if recently qualified)

-
-
-
-

(Name of school, college or university)
(Dates you attended)
(The qualification you achieved)

(Name of school, college or university)
(Dates you attended)
(The qualification you achieved)

(Don't go back further than your senior or secondary school)

(Professional training)

(Details of any professional training undertaken at work)

- (Qualification or skill achieved)
-
-
-
-

Personal details

(Date of birth)
(Driving licence)
(Married or single – only if relevant)
(Nationality – only if relevant)

(Interests and activities. Brief details)

(References – usually 'available on request')

Robert Dalesman
2 Woodland Drive
Sandacre
West Lea
Norfolk NR4 5TE

Tel: 00000 000000
E-mail: rdalesman@anyisp.com

Career profile

A company representative with experience of both sales and distribution with a major company, and the proven ability to meet and surpass sales targets, now keen to move ahead in a challenging sales position with a market leader.

Key strengths

Organisation and initiative: personally responsible for reorganising sales route to reduce costs and maximise profit, increasing turnover by 55 per cent.

Sales, marketing or distribution experience: four years' practical knowledge of sales and distribution; currently completing two-year open learning course covering all aspects of sales and marketing.

Drive and enthusiasm: turned an underperforming route into a highly profitable one. Gained new accounts and developed existing ones by establishing customer needs and preferences. Undertook Certificate in Sales and Marketing in own time and at own expense in order to further career.

Key skills

- Developing customer relationships from cold call to repeat order
- Recognising sales opportunities
- Identifying customer needs
- Organising daily and weekly schedules
- Managing customer credit control and discount negotiation
- Currently working towards Certificate in Sales and Marketing

Career history

Penbury Foods Ltd
2006 to present
Van Sales Representative
Delivered orders to current customers and developed new and existing accounts, including introduction of new lines and products.

Turned a subsidised delivery route into a profit-making sales territory:

- Reorganised two sales routes into one, thereby reducing costs
- Increased turnover by 55% in first six months
- Increased overall turnover by £2,500 per week

Dann Farms Ltd; 2004 to 2006
Customer Deliveries Organiser
Organised weekly schedule of perishable product deliveries to supermarket outlets nationally. Supervised four-man delivery team, and liaised with Transport and Administration Department to coordinate delivery schedules.

Robert Dalesman (cont.)

Lockings Distribution; 1999 to 2004
Van Driver
Part of the Locking Distribution Fleet. Delivered food products to supermarket chains, in accordance with a strict timetable. Maintained daily record logs. Responsible for maintaining vehicle to company standards. Promoted within company from previous position as general loader and driver.

Education and training

Somerston College
1997 to 1999
City and Guilds Warehousing and Distribution

Lea Park School
1992 to 1997
Total of five GCSEs gained, including Maths and English

Professional training

Eastern Institute of Marketing
From September 2007

Certificate in Sales and Marketing
Two-year open learning course covering all aspects of professional sales including:

- Principles of selling
  - pricing and profit
  - negotiation
  - sales promotions
  - sales opportunities
  - advanced selling techniques
  - managing client accounts
  - developing client business
- Managing sales territories
- Finance for sales and marketing
- Law for sales and marketing
- Forecasting and analysis

Personal details

Date of birth:	10 April 1981
Driving licence:	Full, clean UK
Interests:	A keen interest in sport and keeping fit, and play regularly for a local Sunday football team.
References:	Available on request

Include

✓ **Your skills and experience, knowledge and capabilities.** Your relevant experience and competence are the most important things to put in your CV. Match them as closely as possible to those required by the job.

✓ **Skills and qualifications that feature in the job advertisement.** If you are answering an advertised vacancy, or if you have a comprehensive job description, make use of it. This is covered more fully in Chapter 3.

✓ **Your achievements.** A CV is not the place for false modesty: achievements need to be spelled out clearly. Employers rarely have time to search out information, and should be able to see at a glance exactly what you can offer them.

✓ **Put the most important information on the first page.** If your CV runs to two pages, make sure the first page is the most interesting and highlights your key points.

Leave out

✗ **Fussy, unnatural language.** Stick to plain language and clear, unambiguous statements.

✗ **Anything that sounds desperate.** It says, in effect, 'I'll do anything'.

✗ **Unnecessary personal details.** The less irrelevant information there is on the page the more clearly your achievements stand out. Unless you feel they are relevant, you can quite safely leave out the following:

Marital status	Religious affiliation
Maiden name	Political affiliation
Number of children	Age (in addition to date of birth)
Ages of children	Previous salary
Nationality	Reason for leaving last job
Gender	Photographs
Partner's occupation	

✗ **Negative information.** While it's unwise to lie in your CV, you don't have to include information that will diminish your chance of an interview – as long as it doesn't affect your ability to do the job. Always put things in the most positive way that you can.

✗ **Out-of-date and irrelevant information.** Things that happened more than 10 years ago are of very little interest unless they have a direct bearing on your present capabilities. What you are doing currently is much more relevant.

✗ **References.** If references are required, they will be taken up later. There is no need to put the names and addresses of referees on your CV.

Checklist

- **Your finished CV should:**
  - be easy to read;
  - be easy to understand;
  - be attractive;
  - present your skills, strengths and achievements clearly;
  - encourage the reader to want to interview you.
- **The layout of your CV**, the way it is actually arranged on the page, is important. Include:
  - wide margins;
  - clear spacing;
  - discreetly used capital letters and bullet points to emphasise information;
  - short, clearly headed, easy-to-read sections.

When you have written your CV, check the following points:

- ☐ Is the layout clear?
- ☐ Do the relevant points stand out?
- ☐ Is the language clear and understandable?
- ☐ Are your skills and achievements emphasised?
- ☐ Can the employer see the key points at a glance, or does the information have to be searched for and guessed at?
- ☐ Is it free of irrelevant details?
- ☐ Is it free of qualifying words such as fairly, usually and hopefully?
- ☐ Does a positive picture of you emerge?
- ☐ Is it well presented, smart and professional looking?

Finally

When you send your CV, remember the following:

- Always send your CV to a named individual within the company, not just to The Personnel Department. If you don't know the name of the person to send it to, ring up and find out.
- Include a covering letter written specifically to match the requirements of that job.
- The letter should be as well presented as your CV and typed on good-quality, white or cream, A4 paper.
- Send your CV and covering letter unfolded in a white or cream A4 size envelope. Don't try to save on postage by cramming it into a smaller envelope.

- If there is a closing date, make sure your application is sent off in good time. Applications received after the deadline are rarely, if ever, considered.

Any questions?

Should I put it in or leave it out?

There are two basic questions to ask yourself when considering whether or not to put an item of information into your CV:

- Will it encourage them to interview me?
- Will it discourage them from interviewing me?

If the answer to the first question is an emphatic yes, put it in. If, however, you feel less certain, think carefully about including it. Could the space be used more effectively to expand on something more important?

If you answer yes to the second question, leave it out.

2

CVs section by section

Information is easier to digest when it's sorted into small, clearly labelled portions. As you may have already noticed, each CV in this book is divided into clear, easy-to-read sections:

Career profile
Key strengths
Key skills
Career history
Education and training
Personal details

This chapter looks at each section in more detail, with further examples.

Section 1 – the career profile

This is a brief statement that summarises your background and experience. We'll look at this section in great detail in Chapter 3.

Section 2 – key strengths

We'll also look at this in detail in Chapter 3. It is, briefly, a section that highlights the most important skills, experience and personal qualities that make you the right person for the job.

These are the two sections you will customise so that each CV is tailor-made for the job you want.

Meanwhile, let's continue with the rest of your CV so that you have it organised and prepared ready for those final details to be added when you apply for a job.

Section 3 – your key skills

Including a section highlighting your key skills can save anyone reading your CV a lot of time and effort.

The key skills section can be used to summarise and emphasise your:

- key skills and abilities or capabilities;
- key qualifications;
- key achievements.
- (The main skills you have developed)
- (Particularly those appropriate to the job you are applying for)
- ______
- ______
- ______

Key skills

Example 1

- Management and supervision of staff
- An extensive knowledge of purchasing control
- The ability to operate an effective pricing policy
- An understanding of hygiene requirements at all points of contact
- A keen sense of the importance of margins and profits

Example 2

- Keyboard skills – 40 wpm
- Operation of
  - fax machine
  - photocopiers – Canon and Rank Xerox
  - franking machine
- Preparing and writing routine correspondence
- Organising and carrying out routine administrative work
  - maintaining records
  - dealing with incoming telephone calls
  - dealing with incoming mail

Example 3

- Carrying out routine security procedures
- Monitoring security equipment including alarms and surveillance cameras
- Checking and verifying all incoming personnel including deliveries
- Carrying out routine checking and maintenance of safety equipment

Key qualifications

Example 1

- RSA III Typewriting – current speed 70 wpm
- RSA II Audio-typing – current speed 70 wpm
- RSA II Shorthand – current speed 120 wpm
- RSA Certificate in Computer Literacy and Information Technology:
  - Microsoft Office:
    Word
    Excel
    Access

Example 2

- BSc Mechanical Engineering
- Practical experience of programming:
  - CNC machinery
  - CMM
  - Robots
- Use of CAD/CAM systems
- Computer programming languages:
  - C++
  - FORTRAN
  - COBOL

Key achievements

Example 1

- Developing key ranges, many of which reached top ten leading brand status, including:
  - freeze-dried pasta sauces
  - savoury snack rice
  - fresh chilled soups

- Improving processing methods in natural-set department, reducing spoilage and improving profit margins
- Reducing wastage in thick-set yoghurt department with similar effect
- Consistently bringing processing trials in to time and on budget

Example 2

- Initiating design services group specialising in high-quality visual aids and display material, employing a team of eight designers and technicians
- Building up 'blue-chip' client list, including ICL, Hewlett-Packard, SmithKline Beecham, Manpower Services Commission, British Home Stores, Rolls Royce Aerospace
- Producing full marketing packages for London Manchester Insurance Group, ICI, South West Water, among others
- Liaising with Harpen Exhibition Group to produce Eurotech '07 in Brussels

Example 3

- Successfully managing, training and motivating 20 staff in three branches, thereby exceeding targets for insurance, savings, and mortgage lending sales
- Organising and opening two new suburban branch offices, and exceeding forecast transaction levels by 25% in the first year of operation
- Organising full relocation of group departments to new premises within strict deadlines
- Devising and delivering OLE and DDL training to Sales Support staff, enabling them to use data analysis tools; and to Secretarial staff, enabling them to produce presentations, graphs and organisation charts, and to maximise efficient system usage
- Designing and providing user-friendly computer spreadsheet for Commercial Lending Sales Team, enabling them to project lending terms and reduction of capital balances for given varying repayment possibilities

Section 4 – your career history

Your career history tells a prospective employer what you have done and where and when you have done it.

For each entry in your career history section, include:

- the name of the company;
- the dates you worked there;
- your job title or position;
- the main responsibilities of that position;
- your key achievements during your time there.

(**Name of company**, usually starting with the most recent) ________

(Dates you worked there) ________

(Job title) ________

(Brief description of what you did) ________

____

(Brief description of what you achieved in this position) ________

- ________
- ________
- ________

Example 1

K&L Polton
2002 to 2008
Human Resources Manager
Trained, assessed and developed staff at all levels

- Responsible for 750 employees
- Devised and introduced new appraisal system for all departments, based on performance assessment and linked to performance-related pay structure
- Trained in-house assessors for new system

- Initiated use of interactive software for staff development in areas other than IT training
- Supervised a professional training team of 10

Example 2

Axon Business Machines
2002 to 2008
Sales Executive
Appointed to direct sales role. Responsible for meeting targets on sales of office equipment in business-to-business environment. Achievements include:

- Directed highly successful sales team to top company awards
- Increased profit margins by more than 10%
- Won Top Salesperson Award two years in succession
- Achieved more than 100% increase in technical support revenue budgets

Example 3

Safe As Houses
2006 to present
Volunteer Counsellor
Counselled young people with a variety of problems centring on homelessness. Managed a heavy caseload, giving advice and information on housing and benefit entitlements where appropriate, and participated in supervision and support meetings. Attended residential course on Means Tested Benefits by the Welfare Rights Unit.

Example 4

Peel Supplies Ltd
2005 to present
Warehouse and Distribution Supervisor

- Supervised 25 full-time staff, rising to 35 at peak periods
- Instructed and monitored incoming trainees
- Verified and processed orders

- Introduced and established incentive scheme that reduced petty pilfering by 75%
- Promoted from Warehouse Assistant to Warehouse and Distribution Supervisor in 2003

Example 5

Eight 'til Late Shop, Bartonbury
2005 to 2008
Cashier and Kiosk Assistant
General care of stock:

- Checked deliveries
- Replenished shelves
- Ordered stock using computerised system

Cash handling:

- Cashier duties, including balancing tills
- Handled upwards of £5,000 per day

Customer care:

- Served and assisted customers
- Handled enquiries and complaints
- Responsible for alcohol and cigarette legislation

Example 6

The Woodland School Project, Bannham
Summer 2006 and 2008
Drama Instructor
Worked as part of a team to plan and implement out-of-school drama project for 70 mixed-ability students aged 8 to 11. Taught performance techniques, monitored students' progress, maintained records. Coached and motivated to production standard, set goals to encourage performance levels.

Section 5 – your education and training

If you have just left school, college or university, this section will probably take a higher priority and include more detailed information. If, however, you have more than two years' experience of working, your career details will be of more interest to a prospective employer.

Education and training can include:

- academic achievements, diplomas and degrees, etc;
- professional qualifications;
- technical qualifications;
- vocational training where relevant;
- relevant company training programmes;
- computer skills and training;
- language skills;
- professional membership of relevant associations.

(Starting with the highest, most recent OR most relevant qualification) __________

(Name of school, college, or university) __________

(Dates you attended) __________

(The qualification you achieved) __________

(You could include brief details of what was covered in the course, especially if recently qualified) __________

- __________
- __________
- __________
- __________

(Professional training)

(Details of any professional training undertaken at work)

- (Qualification or skill achieved)
-
-
-

Example 1

West Midlands University
2000 to 2003
BSc Computer Science

- Robotics – concepts, VAL, 3-D modelling of component assembly, matrices
- Graphics – 2-D and 3-D, projection, transformation matrices
- Communications – network theory, protocols, hardware
- Database Theory – structure storage, design
- Formal Logic – trinary, fuzzy, temporal
- Artificial Intelligence – Popll, expert systems, Prolog, theory of neural nets

Example 2

2002 University of the South
Postgraduate Diploma in European Business Administration

2000 Institute of Linguists
Institute of Linguists Intermediate Diploma in German

1999 UOS School of Business
RSA Preparatory Certificate Teaching English as a Foreign Language

1998 London Polytechnic
BA Hons English and German Literature 2:1

Example 3

2000–2005 Westbrook College of Further Education
Certificate of Counselling Theory AEB/CAC
Certificate of Counselling Practice AEB/CAC

1997–2000 Forest Community College
Open Access vocational courses:

- Post-Trauma Stress and Critical Incident Debriefing
- Primary Health Care Counselling
- Managing Short-Term Counselling Work within Primary Care
- Women and Mental Health

Example 4

Professional qualifications

2004	Diploma in Marketing	Institute of Marketing
2001	Certified Diploma in Accounting and Finance	Chartered Association of Accountants
1994	Diploma in Management Studies	Westland College
1992	BSc Hons Degree Economics	University of Dorset

Professional training

Computer skills

- Microsoft Office:
  Word
  Access
  Excel
  Powerpoint
  Outlook

Language skills

- Fluent conversational and business German
- Competent spoken French

Member of the Institute of Marketing

Example 5

1996 to 1999 Collworth College of Technology
BTEC HND Food Technology
Access to Science Course

1991 to 1996 Albert Ellis High School
3 A levels: Economics, French, English
5 GCSEs including Maths and English

Section 6 – your personal details

The details often covered in this section include:

Personal details:

- date of birth, if you wish to include it;
- possession of a clean driving licence;
- nationality – if relevant;
- special details such as a registered disability.

Interests and activities:

- brief details of anything that will add to or support the picture of yourself you are presenting.

References:

- usually covered by 'available on request'.

(Date of birth) ____________________

(Driving licence) ____________________

(Nationality – only if relevant) ____________________

(Interests and activities. Brief details) ____________________

____

____

(References – usually 'available on request') ____________________

Example 1

Date of birth:	15 November 1970
Driver:	Car owner, full, clean UK licence
Interests:	Team sports – netball, volleyball. Running. Took part in London Marathon in 2006
References:	Available on request

Example 2

Date of birth:	1 January 1980
Relocation:	Prepared to relocate
Interests:	Reading, singing and writing. I have frequently sung in a professional capacity, and have appeared as an extra for both the BBC and HTV and am a member of Equity. Produced several shows and plays for the local dramatic society.
References:	Available on request.

Example 3

Date of birth:	25 May 1961
Licence:	Full, clean UK driving licence
Health:	Non-smoker
Interests:	All aspects of conservation work including the National Trust for Conservation, World Wide Fund for Nature, and the RSPB. Chair of the local conservation group, and have organised and participated in several local projects.
References:	Available on request.

Your CV should look something like the following when you've finished.

William Edwards
5 Holton Green Road
Stowerbridge
Lancs. LN 4 6TD

Tel: 00000 000000
e-mail: willedwards@anyisp.com

Career profile

Key strengths

Key skills

- Managing accounts and maintaining long-term customer relationships
- Motivating, developing and recruiting staff, including staff training and incentives
- Planning and controlling sales resources to maximum effect
- Maintaining cash flow and profitability
- Analysing and evaluating sales results
- Planning and implementing public relations and advertising campaigns

Career history

Sullivan Centres
2003 to present
Area Manager
Managed Northern region of a national charity:

- Increased funding revenue by 57% over three years
- Took over and re-established area that had fallen into neglect
- Built up team of trained, professional volunteers
- Established efficient collection service
- Produced and implemented marketing plan
- Improved methods of forwarding donations
- Worked towards Institute of Management NVQ level 4

EJK & Sons Ltd
1999 to 2003
Sales/Product Manager
Directly responsible to the Managing Director and Sales and Marketing Director for all aspects relating to promotion and sale of product range:

- Organised and established new product range from concept to completion
- Took over two neglected product ranges and increased turnover by 37%

William Edwards (cont.)

- Organised continuous training programme for internal and external sales personnel with training in sales and product knowledge
- Planned and organised exhibitions and seminars
- Prepared and delivered presentations at all levels including hands-on product demonstrations to groups of all sizes

Utilities (UK) Ltd
1994 to 1999
Product Manager
- Successfully increased sales year on year
- Maintained profitability of product range
- Organised consistently innovative public relations and advertising campaign
- Introduced and marketed new product ranges
- Trained and managed sales team
- Supervised customer orders and oversaw stock control

Bearstrom Ltd
1990 to 1994
Sales Manager
Sales Representative
- Increased sales turnover
- Introduced new products and marketing ideas
- Recruited and trained sales team
- Promoted to Sales Manager in 1992

Education

Institute of Management
2006 to 2008
NVQ Sales and Marketing Management level 4

City Community School
1983 to 1990
- A-levels: Mathematics; Geography
- GCSEs: seven including Maths and English

Personal details

Date of birth:	4 May 1972
Health:	non-smoker
Interests:	Badminton Riding Coach for under-11 football team

Full, clean UK driving licence

References available on request

Any questions?

What if I don't have any achievements?

Does it help to think of them as accomplishments rather than achievements? In every job you've held, you must have accomplished something, had some goal or outcome in mind, otherwise why bother turning up for work each day? Even the most routine jobs offer the chance to learn new skills, interact with others, meet targets, improve your working methods and develop new responsibilities. Read some of the CVs later in this book to give you some ideas and get you thinking.

What if there are gaps in my work record?

If the gaps include voluntary work, training or relevant experience – travel, for example – put these down as part of your skills, qualifications and achievements.

Otherwise, giving the year of employment, rather than month and year, will cover short employment gaps.

Example

Change this...
Career history
Sollbury Ltd
September 2007 to July 2008
Market researcher

Hunt and Covey Retail
August 2005 to January 2007
Retail Assistant

...to this
Career history
Sollbury Ltd
2007 to 2008
Market researcher

Hunt and Covey Retail
2005 to 2007
Retail Assistant

If the gaps are early on in your career history, focus attention on your current position, and very briefly summarise that period of employment:

Various
1996 to 2001
Retail and market research

For solutions to other CV problems, see Chapter 5.

3

The tailor-made CV

If you were beginning to wonder what to do with those first two sections on your CV – the Career profile and Key strengths – this is the chapter that lets you into the secret. They are your opportunity to tailor your CV so that each application you make addresses the specific needs and requirements of that employer.

Recruitment these days is a matter of competency and fit. Companies go to great lengths to establish the competencies required for each job; that is, the knowledge, skills, personal qualities and experience that mean that you will be able to do that job. When a vacancy is advertised, the ad is often based on those core competencies. When the CVs come in, companies look at applicants to see if they are a good fit – how well does what's being offered match what they've said they want? Candidates with the CVs that demonstrate the best fit are the ones who are picked for interview.

To make your CV stand out, you need to offer the best fit possible. A sure-fire way to do so is to write your Career profile and your Key strengths sections afresh each time so that they reflect the exact requirements of the job.

Emphasising your good fit by highlighting it in a separate section saves the employer the bother of having to search out the information for themselves from the rest of your CV. Some competencies are very specific, anyway. Would you go into detail about your ability to 'put clients at their ease' or 'build reciprocal customer relationships' in a non-tailored CV? Yet if that's what the employer is asking for, that's what you need to give them.

To do this, you need to do some homework before completing your CV and sending it off.

Read the job ad

Many job advertisements will tell you a lot about what to put in your CV. As well as the local and national press and online sites, the best place to look for advertised vacancies is in the journals and magazines associated with your particular trade or profession. When you find an ad for a job you want, study it with a view to using the information in it. You need to answer the following questions:

- What is the purpose of the job?
- What is the value of the job to the company?
- What are the crucial competencies? (Skills, knowledge, qualifications, experience?)
- What are the desirable competencies?
- What sort of person are they looking for?

The first two questions help you to focus on the job requirements and put them in context; the rest of the questions focus on specific requirements.

Personal Assistant

A small private publisher urgently requires a mature, hard-working assistant to provide administrative and secretarial support. Must have excellent communication and organisational abilities. Keyboard skills (Microsoft Office suite currently used) and a confident telephone

> manner essential. Experienced bookkeeper familiar with spreadsheets would be an advantage but training will be given to the right applicant. Understanding of environmental issues desirable. Must be able to work on own initiative without supervision and have a flexible approach to working hours.

What is the purpose of the job?

To provide secretarial, administrative and organisational support to a small private publisher (probably concerned with environmental issues), including bookkeeping and answering the phone.

What is the value of the job to the company?

Competent, efficient administrative support ensures that the publisher can do his or her job unhindered; a professional face is presented to the world (preparing letters and answering the phone); business records and data are organised, which means they can be accessed, retrieved and used easily.

What are the crucial competencies? (Skills, knowledge, qualifications, experience?)

Computer skills – preferably Microsoft Office; secretarial and admin experience; communication skills including confident phone manner; organisational abilities; initiative, ie the ability to plan and prioritise.

What are the desirable competencies?

Some bookkeeping experience; familiarity with spreadsheets (Excel if they use Microsoft Office); **or** someone able and willing to undergo training; an understanding of environmental issues.

What sort of person are they looking for?

Someone with a confident, mature, professional attitude; self-motivated and experienced enough to work on their own initiative without constant supervision; willing to learn new skills; interested in the environment; flexible (not a nine-to-five person). Someone used to routine office work but able to cope with responsibility and the unexpected when it arises.

Now take an ad for a job you'd like to apply for and go through the same questions. Write down the answers – don't try to keep them all in your head; you need to be able to look at them on paper.

When you have your answers, the first things to ask yourself are: is this the sort of job I want, and am I that sort of person with those particular skills and qualities?

Look for other information

Before you get on to customising your CV, look around for any other background information you can find about the job and the company. Knowledge is power, and the more you know, the more empowered you become.

The job description

Quite often, ads ask you to contact the company for more information. Always do so, because they will often send you useful things like company information and a comprehensive job description for the vacancy. This will give you even more detail about the duties and responsibilities of the job and the required competencies.

The company website

Look up the company home page on the internet for information about the sort of company they are: what they do, what sort of image they have, what sort of clients they have and so on. As well as straightforward factual information, get as much of a feel for the company as you can.

Annual reports and company brochures

Most companies will send copies of these to you if you ask.

Articles

Put the company name into a search engine to see what comes up.

Professional profiles

Look up the sort of job you want on career sites and on professional association sites and chat rooms. These can give you an overview of the key requirements and alert you to what the current issues are.

Use the information to customise your CV

You're now ready to complete the remaining two sections on your CV: the Career profile and Key strengths.

Career profile

You can use that company information to write a Career profile that emphasises just how good a fit your current situation, background and future requirements are with the company you are applying to.

This Career profile was written to reflect the requirements of the job ad on page 32:

Career profile

Highly experienced and reliable Personal Assistant with full Microsoft Office training, current experience of working in an exceptionally busy office and a background in customer relations. Now looking for a position where a wide spectrum of secretarial, administrative and organisational skills can be used to the full providing comprehensive support for a worthwhile organisation.

As you can see, a Career profile is a short statement that gives a summary of who you are, what you do and what you are aiming for with your application. It needs to be as succinct as possible while still including:

- who you are – your job title; professional status; background;
- what you can offer – your skills; experience; knowledge;
- what you've achieved – what you most want the employer to know about you; the unique combination of skills, knowledge and experience that makes you right for this job;
- what you want next – the role you want and why; the sort of company you want to work for; the opportunities you would relish.

The applicant in the example above has thought about which aspects of her background and experience would be most useful, what skills would be required, what the job she's applying for would entail and what sort of company she would be doing it for and tailored her Career profile accordingly.

Each of the following profiles was similarly written with a specific job and company in mind.

A professional and highly skilled Retail Manager with six years' experience in high-street retail and a thorough understanding of how to maximise turnover through stock rotation and P&L monitoring. A sales professional with a sound commitment to customer focus and the management skills needed to motivate a sales team to exceed sales targets three years running. Now looking for a position with a recognised leader in the field where these skills can be used to achieve quality results and the highest level of customer satisfaction.

Youth Worker with NVQ level 4 in Advice and Guidance and four years' experience in the community working face to face with young people, helping them to overcome social and economic disadvantages. As someone passionate about diversity and inclusion, I am currently seeking a similarly challenging role where I can make full use of my skills and practical experience to help service users solve problems, overcome barriers and implement effective solutions.

A highly experienced, MBA-qualified Export Manager with eight years' track record of success in export sales, providing high-quality solutions to technical problems and achieving a 27 per cent growth in sales over three years. With a background in engineering and experience of selling into several industry sectors including telecommunications, I am currently interested in a decision-making role with a leading-edge organisation offering the opportunity to further develop excellent management skills and contribute to company growth.

Office Supervisor with four years' experience of organising data and records and the tried and tested ability to maintain a consistently high standard of work and attention to detail under pressure, and to motivate staff to do the same. I am now looking for a challenging work environment where recently updated and enhanced computer skills can be put to good use ensuring the efficient working of a busy and demanding department.

Graphic Designer with HND, three years' experience and first-rate skills in using OSX, Creative Suite 3, Photoshop and Illustrator. Experienced at taking client briefs through to finished artwork, including brochures, advertising and point-of-sale material, and member of the team that won the Indesign Pro award this year. Now looking for the opportunity to join a fast-moving, highly skilled team working on some of the world's most exciting brand names.

Key strengths

In this section you need to demonstrate that you have the competencies – the skills, personal qualities, knowledge and experience that mean you can do the job – that the company requires. It's a simple matter of looking at what they want and telling them what you've got. You need to support your statements, though. It's not enough just to say you have a particular skill, quality or knowledge; you have to back it up with some sort of evidence.

Keep your statements short and succinct and tailor them to fit the job you are applying for.

This Key strengths section was written to reflect the requirements of the job ad on page 32:

Key strengths

Excellent IT and secretarial skills: four years' secretarial experience providing support for two department heads and an Assistant Director. College trained and fully proficient in Microsoft Office; including Word and Excel; currently using Windows XP.

Communication skills: as PA to Assistant Director, excellent presentation required, both verbal and written, as is the ability to liaise effectively with clients and other members of staff in person, by letter and over the phone. As customer relations clerk, handled incoming calls courteously, diplomatically and efficiently.

Initiative and flexibility: currently required to prioritise own workload and manage day-to-day administrative organisation effectively. Sales drives and conferences mean working competently and resourcefully under pressure to tight deadlines to meet urgent requirements. Always happy to 'go the extra mile' when necessary.

If you'd written the job ad on page 32, how could you *not* interview this applicant? Note that she doesn't claim to have bookkeeping experience, although she has been trained to use Excel, a spreadsheet program; nor does she labour her understanding of environmental issues, although she will put in her Personal details that she is a member of the local conservation group and will also include this information in her covering letter. If she had a strong understanding – held an appropriate degree or was actively involved in environmental issues – this information might have been put in her Key strengths section. If an understanding had been essential rather than desirable, details would *have* to be there.

There are more examples of Key strengths sections in the CVs throughout this book.

When you've completed your customised Career profile and Key strengths, go back through the job ad. Is there any information there that you haven't used? Any skills, qualities or experience you haven't mentioned? Any personal characteristics you haven't talked about? If you went through the ad with a red pen and crossed out every word and phrase you've addressed, just about all that should be left is the odd 'and' and 'the'.

The rest of your CV

The rest of your CV needs to support everything you've said in these two sections. After completing them, check over the rest of your CV to see if it needs strengthening in any way. Are there other duties or responsibilities that would be appropriate for the job you're applying for? Are there irrelevancies that could be taken out? Do you have relevant achievements that should be mentioned to support your Career profile and Key strengths?

William Edwards' completed tailor-made CV will follow shortly. First, here's the job ad it was written for:

Fundraising Director, International Medical Charity

We are looking for a Fundraising Director to join a dynamic team concerned with raising money for an internationally recognised medical charity. This is a hands-on role whose purpose is to lead and manage the fundraising team, effectively generating income from major donors, private individuals, trusts and foundations and businesses in the UK and internationally.

The successful candidate will have strong leadership skills and a track record in Fundraising or Sales/Marketing with the emphasis on face-to-face income generation along with team leadership and management. Applicants should be able to generate income through relationship creation, development and excellent presentation. You should be willing to travel within the UK and abroad.

If you feel you meet these criteria, please send your CV to Irene Lowel at __________.

William has taken his prepared CV on pages 26–27 and completed the first two sections – his Career profile and Key strengths – using the information in the job ad to focus his ideas.

William Edwards
5 Holton Green Road
Stowerbridge
Lancs LN4 6TD

Tel: 00000 000000
e-mail: willedwards@anyisp.com

Career profile

Area Manager with a major UK charity with a professional background in sales and marketing. Solid experience of fundraising, working with trusts and foundations as well as businesses and individuals, and of training and motivating a highly successful team to achieve unprecedented results. Now looking for a role where a knowledge and understanding of the business of charity can be used to good effect.

Key strengths

Successful track record in fundraising: six years' experience of upgrading a neglected, underperforming area into a major contributor with a 57 per cent increase in funding based on substantial relationship-building skills developed over more than a decade in sales and marketing.

Presentation skills: currently required to give effective yet enjoyable talks and presentations to the public, the media and other interested bodies to raise awareness and secure donations. Donations last year totalled £3.5 million.

Strong leadership skills: a track record of over 10 years of motivating teams to set and achieve challenging targets and expect the very best from themselves. Feedback from teams demonstrates a vigorous style of leadership based on sincere consultation allied with clear direction and a solid understanding of marketing techniques.

Key skills

- Maintaining long-term customer relationships
- Motivating, developing and recruiting staff, including staff training and incentives
- Planning and controlling resources to maximum effect
- Maintaining cash flow and profitability
- Analysing and evaluating results
- Planning and implementing public relations and advertising campaigns

Career history

Sullivan Centres
2003 to present
Area Manager
Managed Northern region of a national charity:

- Increased funding revenue by 57% over three years
- Took over and re-established area that had fallen into neglect
- Built up team of trained, professional volunteers
- Established efficient collection service
- Produced and implemented marketing plan
- Improved methods of forwarding donations
- Worked towards Institute of Management NVQ level 4

William Edwards (cont.)

EJK & Sons Ltd
1999 to 2003
Sales/Product Manager
Directly responsible to the Managing Director and Sales and Marketing Director for all aspects relating to promotion and sale of product range:

- Organised and established new product range from concept to completion
- Took over two neglected product ranges and increased turnover by 37%
- Organised continuous training programme for internal and external sales personnel with training in sales and product knowledge
- Planned and organised exhibitions and seminars
- Prepared and delivered presentations at all levels, including hands-on product demonstrations to groups of all sizes

Utilities (UK) Ltd
1994 to 1999
Product Manager
- Successfully increased sales year on year
- Maintained profitability of product range
- Organised consistently innovative public relations and advertising campaign
- Introduced and marketed new product ranges
- Trained and managed sales team
- Supervised customer orders and oversaw stock control

Bearstrom Ltd
1990 to 1994
Sales Manager
Sales Representative
- Increased sales turnover
- Introduced new products and marketing ideas
- Recruited and trained sales team
- Promoted to Sales Manager in 1992

Education

Institute of Management
2006 to 2008
NVQ Sales and Marketing Management level 4

City Community School
1983 to 1990
- A-levels: Mathematics; Geography
- GCSEs: seven including Maths and English

Personal details

Date of birth: 4 May 1972
Health: non-smoker
Interests: Badminton
Riding
Coach for under-11 football team

Full, clean UK driving licence
References available on request

Any questions?

What if there's isn't enough information in the job ad?

By the time you've applied for several jobs, you'll probably find that you're putting some Key strengths in most of the time. When an ad just more or less gives a job title and asks you to apply, these are the Key strengths to use. Find out what you can about the company and make use of the information as we looked at above, and use your intuition and job knowledge to deduce what other strengths they might need, or look at the requirements for a range of jobs with the same or similar job title on a recruitment site such as monster.co.uk.

What if I'm not applying for an advertised vacancy?

If you're making speculative approaches – sending your CV to companies that haven't yet advertised a vacancy – then use the same techniques as above. Customise your Career profile to suit the company you're approaching and use your knowledge and experience to work out what skills and qualities they would most value.

If you're posting your CV on a recruitment site or sending out a mass CV mailing, then either decide what sort of company you want to work for and put that in your Career profile or leave that part out altogether and just focus on who you are and what you've done.

I've looked at the job description and it lists 10 competencies. Do I have to address all of them?

Pick out the two or three that make this job different from all the others and put these in your Key strengths section, or pick the ones you know to be the most valuable and sought-after. Mention the others in your Key skills or under achievements in your work history, but make sure that they go in somewhere.

Why do I have to customise my CV; can't all this go in my covering letter?

Yes, it can go in your covering letter and it should, but it needs to go in your CV as well. Use your covering letter to say why you are applying for this particular job with this particular company and point out what a good match your skills and experience are for the requirements of the job. Use the same sources that you used to customise your CV but don't just repeat the information, rephrase it and try to come up with a fresh angle. (For lots more information on what to write and how to write it, see the companion book to this one, *Readymade Job Search Letters.*)

However, your covering letter can become detached from your CV; your CV can be filed without the letter; your CV can be scanned into a bank minus the letter; your CV can be passed on to HR or a department head without the letter. . . better by far to have the most important information – your suitability for the job – actually on your CV, where there is no chance it can get lost or be overlooked.

4

The computer-friendly CV

How things have changed

The advances in computer technology and developments in the workplace mean that application procedures have changed in significant ways. In particular, we've seen the increased use of computers to:

- advertise job vacancies on the internet;
- facilitate online job applications;
- provide access to CV banks;
- scan and store CVs in databases;
- scan CVs to pre-select likely candidates.

This means that, these days, a computer-friendly CV is essential for any serious job seeker.

How the internet can help

One of the key reasons for computer-proofing your CV is so you can get maximum benefit from using the internet. Over the past few years, the internet has become a major job-search tool. This significant means of communication offers the opportunity to:

- obtain information about companies and employers;
- discover the jobs on offer;
- contact potential employers promptly;
- boost the scale and speed of your applications;
- network with newsgroups;
- get your CV in front of many more recruiters;
- post your CV in a variety of CV banks;
- scan job banks;
- find and apply for a wide variety of opportunities.

Other advantages of applying online are:

- Your application arrives in perfect condition.
- It arrives promptly without being delayed in the post.
- It couldn't be cheaper – a particular consideration if you're applying for jobs abroad.

If you find a suitable vacancy on the internet – whether at an employer's website or through a recruitment site – consider applying electronically rather than on paper unless it asks specifically for a paper application. If an employer is advertising on the internet, it could mean they want someone who is at ease with it. Replying in the same medium says that you are the computer-literate employee they are looking for. You can either fill in an online form or e-mail a CV with covering letter.

Online job hunting can be quick and convenient, but the ground rules are the same as for any other sort of approach: you need to stand out from the crowd.

Is your CV computer-friendly?

There are two things to consider when computer-proofing your CV: are both the online version and the paper version scanner-friendly, and can you make it internet-friendly?

Is it scanner-friendly?

Even paper CVs received through the mail are often scanned into a computer database for easy storage and access. Make it easy for an optical scanner to read yours:

- Use plain white or cream paper.
- Print on one side only.
- Use a standard, clear, common font.
- Use 12-point print.
- Send a fresh print, not a photocopy.
- Don't staple or paper-clip pages together.
- Don't fold your CV or the scanner may try to read the fold line. Send it in an A4 envelope.
- Italics, script, graphics, underlining and so on confuse some scanning packages. Keep your text as plain and as clear as possible. Save bold print for section headings.
- Put your name on a separate line at the top of each page – not just the first one – in case the scan is interrupted or becomes corrupted.

Increasingly, large organisations that receive a lot of applications for jobs – through the post or internet – or that search vast online CV banks, cut down on time and work by making an initial electronic scan. They use software that carries out an initial selection based on keyword searches. If your CV passes this first scan, it's passed on to a human adjudicator for further consideration. Make sure your CV doesn't fall at the first fence by including those vital keywords – see below.

Is it internet-friendly?

When you send your CV to an employer by e-mail, there are a number of points that have to be taken into consideration:

- A screen is much smaller than a sheet of A4 paper.
- Only one section can be seen initially.
- E-mail is often read more quickly and with less attention than conventional letters.
- You may be competing for attention with many other e-mails.
- Your CV may be sent on or forwarded to others.
- Your CV and covering letter may initially be scanned by software rather than a person.

This means that:

- You have only a small window of opportunity in which to persuade the recruiter to read your CV.
- What the person sees on the screen first will decide whether he or she reads the rest or not.
- Every line counts – even the subject line.
- Keywords are important.

You also need to bear in mind that if you put your CV in a CV bank it may be just one of many very similar ones sitting and waiting for scanning software to pick it out.

The importance of keywords

Keywords are important in all CVs, but especially so when computerised selection procedures are involved. Any CV needs to grab the reader's attention, but it's even more of a problem when the attention you're trying to grab isn't even human – just a program designed to look for specific words or phrases.

Keywords include:

- **Positions** – manager, programmer, editor, engineer, director.
- **Occupational background** – teaching, engineering, public relations, retailing, financial management, quality control, customer care, sales and marketing.
- **Knowledge areas** – capacity planning, policy and procedures, interactive technology, systems configuration, project planning, budget and resource management, MIS management, conceptual design, global markets, product development, restructuring, crisis resolution, sales and distribution.
- **Specific skills and qualifications** – Microsoft Word, Windows NT, ISO 9000, BSc, MA, two years' experience of. . .
- **Workplace skills** – designed, evaluated, represented, organised, formulated, developed.

The keywords in this extract from a CV are highlighted in bold, and the type of keyword is indicated in italics:

Example

Customer Service Manager (*position*)
C&G **Telecommunications** (*background*) – 2004 to Present

Supervised (*workplace skill*) divisional **customer service** (*background*) staff:

- **Organised** (*workplace skill*) **staff schedules** (*knowledge area*)
- **Trained** (*workplace skill*) staff in **customer care** (*knowledge area*)
- **Implemented** (*workplace skill*) new **policy procedures** (*knowledge area*)
- **Monitored** (*workplace skill*) service to ensure **targets and objectives** (*knowledge area*) met
- Used **Windows XP** (*specific skill*) with **Access** (*specific skill*) for customer **database** (*knowledge area*)

Study the job advertisement or the job description carefully when you compose your CV and extract the keywords as a starting point.

- **Be specific.** If the job description asks for word processing skills, state the specific skills you have – Word, PowerPoint, Outlook, etc. If you are, for example, a manager or a designer, say what you have managed or what you designed.
- **Go into detail.** If you are an IT professional with a range of skills and experience, give details of what exactly those skills and experience are:
  - Four years' experience in IT Development
  - Experience in Unix Operating System
  - Worked as an ORACLE DBA
  - Wrote reports using Report Writer 2x
  - Worked as part of a project team.

The internet-friendly CV

Much of the advice about writing CVs applies just as much to those sent via the internet or stored in CV banks or databases as to any other. In particular:

- Keep it short and concise.
- Keep it simple so the important information stands out.
- Keep it clear and easy to read.
- Keep it relevant.

When you send your CV by e-mail, though, there are a few specific points that don't necessarily apply to CVs sent through the post.

Sending your CV

You can either send your CV as a file attached to an e-mail, or put it in the main body of the text. Sending your CV as an attached file, though, could be a problem. Because of the threat of viruses, many organisations are wary of opening files from an unknown source. Put it in the main body of your e-mail instead. Save your existing word-processed CV as a Rich Text file, then edit and paste it into the e-mail composition box.

The subject line

Always fill in the subject line. If you reply to an advertised vacancy, put the job title and any reference number. If you are making a speculative application, put something appropriate, but make it clear and concise. It may be tempting to try to intrigue with a 'teaser' subject line, but you run the risk of causing irritation when the real purpose of your e-mail becomes clear. Instead, try to include those important keywords:

Subject: Office Manager – City Executive Assistant interested
Subject: Ref 311 Financial Administrator – FCMA 7 years' exp.
Subject: Job ref 2889 – MBA interested
Subject: Marketing exec Ref 446 – New York/London experience offered

Covering letter

Follow with a brief summary of the most important points of your CV – your achievements, skills and experience. Keep in mind that if what appears on the screen doesn't impress, the rest of your e-mail probably won't be read:

> Project Manager – IT experienced
> Jane Smith [jsmith@anyisp.com]
> To: 'Jane Phillips (jphillips@abc.com)'
>
> Dear Ms Phillips
> I would like to apply for the post of Senior Project Manager (Ref 771) as detailed on Jobs.com.
>
> My achievements include:
> - developing three multi-million-pound projects
> - increasing Nestor penetration of IT sector by 15%
> - increasing the market share of Highmatch by 10%
> - increasing Highmatch profits by 8%.
>
> I have an excellent track record in project management, particularly information technology, having worked for major companies in the field.
>
> My full CV follows.

Layout and appearance

Details

Your name, e-mail address and the date already appear at the top of the page. Start the main body of your CV – your Personal Statement followed by your Key Skills/Experience – immediately rather than take up valuable screen space with your home address and telephone number. Put these at the end of your CV instead.

Fonts

Use standard fonts for e-mailed CVs. If you use a font the recipient does not have, your CV could be unreadable.

Screen size

An e-mail screen is much smaller than a sheet of A4 paper – it only displays about 20–25 lines at the most. The first screen that comes up will also have your name, e-mail address and subject details at the top, which leaves even less space – about 10 lines – for the key information that will make an employer want to read further. Bear this in mind when planning your CV.

You will need to edit your CV so that it still looks good on the small screen:

- Make it as short and concise as possible. A CV that takes up just two A4 pages can run to six or seven on e-mail.
- Arrange information in bite-size – or, rather, screen-size – chunks so that it appears in one easy-to-assimilate piece on-screen.
- Don't rely on formatting tools – bullets, bold, italics and so on. Some recipients will only be able to view e-mail in plain text. Use capital letters and spacing instead to set out the information clearly.

- However, if you know for certain that your recipient can receive HTML format, you can incorporate your CV as it appears in your word-processed copy, complete with bullet points, borders, assorted fonts and the like.
- Get an employer's view of your CV: look at it in the outbox before sending it off.

It is relatively straightforward to adapt your standard CV so that it still looks good even in plain text. The following example shows one that has been changed from formatted to plain text for e-mail.

Changing a CV – an example

Original word-processed CV:

Angela Walker
31 Pollard Way
Marsh Cross
Cambridge
CM14 2KL

Tel: 00000 000000
e-mail: awalker@anyisp.com

Personal profile

A highly motivated school leaver with experience of office work. Punctual, reliable and willing to learn, with a good basic education and a strong aptitude for organisation and administration.

Key skills

Keyboard skills – 40 wpm
Operating
- fax machine
- photocopiers – Canon and Rank Xerox
- franking machine

Preparing and writing routine correspondence
Organising and carrying out routine administrative work
Maintaining records
Dealing with incoming telephone calls
Dealing with incoming and outgoing mail

Work experience

Summer 2008
Ashbourn & Sedley
Office Assistant

2007–2008
Marsh Cross School Administration Department
Administrative Assistant (part-time/voluntary)

Education

2001–2008 Marsh Cross School
GCSE

- English language
- English literature
- Maths
- French
- History
- Economics

RSA Stage I Keyboard Skills
RSA Stage I Office Skills
ICT training

Personal details

Date of birth: 30 March 1990
Interests: Riding and pony-trekking, reading and cinema

CV changed to plain text for e-mail (for direct application without a covering letter)

Office Assistant application
Angela Walker [awalker@anyisp.com]
To: 'Paul Rogers (progers@mediapress.co.uk'

Highly motivated school leaver with experience of office work.
Punctual, reliable and willing to learn, with a good basic education and a strong aptitude for organisation and administration.

KEY SKILLS
~ Keyboard skills – 40wpm
~ Fax machine
~ Photocopiers – Canon and Rank Xerox
~ Franking machine

ADMINISTRATIVE SKILLS
~ Preparing and writing routine correspondence
~ Organising and performing administrative tasks
~ Maintaining records
~ Dealing with incoming telephone calls
~ Dealing with incoming and outgoing mail
---------------------------this is roughly the end of the first screen

WORK EXPERIENCE
Summer 2008
Ashbourn & Sedley
~ Office Assistant
2007–2008
Marsh Cross School Administration Department
~ Administrative Assistant (part-time/voluntary)

EDUCATION
2001–2008 Marsh Cross School
GCSE
~ English language
~ English literature
~ Maths
~ French
~ History
~ Economics
RSA Stage I Keyboard Skills
RSA Stage I Office Skills
ICT training

PERSONAL DETAILS
Date of birth: 30 March 1990
Interests: Riding and pony-trekking, reading and cinema
Address: 31 Pollard Way, Marsh Cross, Cambridge CM14 2KL
Tel: 00000 000000

Online application forms

If you reply to an advertised vacancy on an employer's website or recruitment site, the application form may be set up for you already – all you have to do is fill in the blanks. There are drawbacks to ready-prepared application forms, though. They are designed to obtain standard information and don't allow much flexibility about how you present it. If your particular skills and abilities don't stack up neatly in boxes, search out employers who prefer a CV.

Some specific things to remember when you fill in application forms online:

- Read the instructions carefully before you start.
- Don't fill in the application form online and shoot it off straight away. As with any other application, take time to think about it. You probably won't have a spellchecker available, so check everything very carefully. Where possible, cut and paste your existing (already spell-checked) plain-text CV into the form to avoid errors.
- Make full use of any hints, tips and advice the site offers. Many offer a considerable amount.
- Fill in all the boxes – incomplete forms are often not accepted.
- As with your CV, make the information you put in as relevant as possible to the job you are applying for.
- Remember to look for and include those keywords.

Protecting your privacy

Lack of privacy is one possible disadvantage with online job hunting. Using workplace facilities to carry out your job search presents potential problems, while posting your CV with a job bank means anyone can see it – including the organisation you currently work for. When an unobtrusive job search is vital, remember:

- Employers can legally read your mail and track your internet use, so don't send e-mails from your workplace PC or have them sent to you there. You shouldn't do this anyway unless you have the permission of your employer.
- You wouldn't give your workplace phone number in these circumstances, so don't give your workplace e-mail address either. Use your home address or set up a separate account accessible from outside.

- Before enrolling, check what privacy protection your chosen CV bank provides. Many have password protection, visitor screening and so on to ensure discretion.
- Recruiters understand if you don't include names on your CV. You can call yourself 'Job Seeker' or 'Experienced Accountant', etc. Instead of the name of your current employer you can put 'a major company', 'a financial organisation', 'a South West Engineering Company' or something similar.

General points

Take as much time and care with your online CV as you would with any other:

- Check the spelling and grammar thoroughly.
- Present it as attractively and as clearly as possible.
- Find out who can make the decision and send it to that person.
- Send speculative CVs individually and resist the temptation of copying them to a dozen other people at the same time.
- If you are sending your CV as an attached file, remember to include your own name in the file name, such as johnsmithcv.doc. An organisation could receive several dozen files just called cv.doc.
- Your e-mail address should be as businesslike as the rest of your presentation. If yours is more like partyanimal@cooldude.com, either change it or set up a separate address just for business.

Any questions?

How do I change my CV into a plain-text one?

Copy your formatted CV (eg laid out with bullet-points, heading in bold print, etc.) into a new file. Convert what you see into plain text: take out all the bullet points, bold headings, underlining, italics and anywhere you've used 'tab' to indent. Change the font to a basic one such as Courier 12 point which should translate into all e-mail systems.

Now reformat it so that it still looks reasonable. Make full use of spaces, capitals, asterisks, etc to achieve a reasonably presentable CV. Don't use any character that doesn't appear on your keyboard, and don't use the word-wrap feature, use 'enter' to create line breaks.

Save the file as a text-only document (ie mycv.txt). If you want to see how well it performs, open the file in Notepad (Windows' text editor) instead of Word and make any further necessary adjustments.

5

Problems, problems

Overcoming problems is often a matter of emphasising some sections of your CV and playing down others. This chapter looks at how this applies to 20 of the most common problems in CV writing.

Problem 1. 'My CV would fill four pages, at least'

The things you have done recently are more important to a prospective employer than things you did years ago. Highlight the skills that are most relevant to the job you are applying for. Detail your recent experience and summarise everything else.

Example

Career profile *(Give a brief career summary)*
A skilled engineer with over 20 years' manufacturing experience in the engineering and furniture industries, including 10 years at senior management level. Currently developing a competitively driven organisation demanding high standards of performance.

Key skills *(Choose the most relevant ones)*

- Operations and manufacturing management
- Logistics management using current tools and techniques
- Staff management: development and management of change strategy
- Financial management control, budget preparation
- Project management

Career history *(Go into detail about your current job. . .)*
Pitman Ltd, Limpsfield
2004 to present
Operations Manager
Responsible for factories and staff within Operations Group

- Reorganised profile business and set up Logistics Support Centre, reducing operating costs by £150k
- Coordinated and managed activities in five factories and Logistics Support Centre, ensured effective running of operations supplying products to customers
- Formulated and implemented change programme in three factories to bring them level with rest of group
- Improved industrial relations, restoring management leadership with help of Partnership Agreement
- Increased financial performance of group by £300k overall
- Promoted to present position from Factory Manager 2006

Vollens Engineering, Stoke
1997 to 2004
Industrial Engineer *(. . . briefly summarise earlier, less relevant ones)*
Industrial engineering services at factory and divisional level. Provided production engineering service with particular emphasis on product costing, value engineering, pre-production engineering and methods improvement.

Problem 2. 'I've just left school/ college/university. What do I put in my CV?'

This topic is covered fully in Chapter 6.

Problem 3. 'My work history isn't straightforward'

If you have a wide range of skills, select those that are the most appropriate to the job you are applying for. Summarise the main themes of your career history in the Profile at the top of your CV and pick appropriate examples to illustrate your Key strengths. Organise the skills and experience you have acquired into groupings under appropriate headings, so that the full range of your skills is covered.

Example

Career profile *(Emphasise any common threads or themes in your career that are relevant to the job you're applying for)*
Sales and management professional with eight years' experience of customer-focused business including retail, telesales, commercial and face-to-face selling as well as business and staff management.
(What do all the jobs have in common? In this case, they're all customer-focussed)

Key skills
Sales

- Maintaining and servicing existing accounts while developing new territory
- Liaising with distribution department to ensure efficient service to customers

- Developing new sales drive offering extended range of products to existing customers
- Producing quarterly analysis of sales by product and customer for head office records

Business management

- Managing businesses, including a busy town centre café, requiring a range of skills, including:
  - Purchasing stock
  - Establishing pricing structures
  - Marketing and promotion
  - Bookkeeping
  - Managing staff

Career history *(If your work history is confusing, summarise it briefly)*

2006–present	Sales Representative	Bullseye Windows, Deanleigh
2004–2006	Manager	Corner's Cafe, Penbury
2000–2004	Manager	Dilly's Gifts, Fosbury
1998–2000	Sales Assistant	Dean Catering, Deansgate
1998	Telesales Representative	Homer Ltd, Penbury
1994–1998	Cellerman and foodstoreman	Foss Hotel, Fosbury

Problem 4. 'I'm doing more than one job'

This situation is becoming more and more common as people adapt to different career structures. You may be doing two part-time jobs instead of one full-time one, or you may be self-employed and also doing a part-time job, or a 'portfolio' worker with several strings to your bow, or a full-timer working on freelance contracts in your own time.

As shown in Problem 3 above, summarise the main theme of your career in a Profile, and organise your range of skills and experience under separate headings. When you come to your Career history, group your jobs together under the relevant date.

Example

Career history
2006 to present
Video Maker
Community Production Facility

- Planned, produced and directed seven 30–60 minute videos for The Parenting Initiative
- Decided with featured experts content and presentation of video
- Planned lighting, camera angles, camera shots
- Designed, produced and directed two independent video shorts

Radio Producer and Presenter
Valley Radio

- Researched, planned and presented weekly community arts slot on local radio
- Delivered reports
- Selected, approached and interviewed guests

Video Trainer/Facilitator
Kids TV
Community Youth Group

- Assisted youth group making youth and community videos
- Trained them in use of video equipment and basics of production and editing
- Coordinated sound, content and storyline

Problem 5. 'I've had a lot of jobs'

Condense your employment record, focusing attention on the skills you have achieved through your experience, and only giving details of your most recent and most relevant positions. Jobs held more than 10 or 15 years ago can often be lumped together as 'various'.

Example

Employment record

2004–present	Logistica Ltd, Gwent **Production Manager**
1996–2004	Owen Pearson, Gwent **Factory Manager** **Industrial Engineer (promoted 1998)**
1990–1996	Various **Engineering and supervisory**

Problem 6. 'I'm changing careers'

Use the Career profile at the head of your CV to make your new direction clear. Pick out your skills, qualities and achievements that are most appropriate to your new career and emphasise these, and give relevant examples in your Key strengths.

Example

Career profile

Qualified counsellor with experience of working with young people under demanding conditions, looking to use and expand existing skills in a challenging and worthwhile situation where there is an opportunity for further development.

Key qualifications

- Certificate of Counselling Practice (AEB)
- Certificate of Counselling Theory (AEB)

Career history
Volunteer Counsellor
Safe As Houses
2005 to present
Counselled young people with a variety of problems centring on homelessness. Managed a heavy caseload, giving advice and information on housing and benefit entitlements where appropriate, and participated in supervision and support meetings. Attended residential course on Means Tested Benefits by the Welfare Rights Unit.

Sales Receptionist
SAR TV & Video Rentals
2004 to 2008
Demonstrated, sold and arranged rentals of TVs and videos, handled cash and security, stock control, telephone enquiries and customer accounts.

Problem 7. 'My relevant experience is in voluntary/unpaid work'

Voluntary positions are acceptable as part of your career history. See the example in Problem 6, above. The skills and experience you have gained from the job are as important as those gained from paid employment. Include them.

Problem 8. 'I haven't got much experience for the job I want to do'

Make the most of what you can offer. Look at your qualifications, training, current experience – including both paid and unpaid work – and personal qualities. Make full use of the Key skills section, along with a Key achievement or Key experience section, which ever seems appropriate, to highlight everything that matches the job you want. Don't leave potential employers to dig these important details out of your CV for themselves.

If lack of experience is a serious handicap, consider 'alternative' ways of getting it, such as volunteering, an unpaid work-experience placement, temporary or part-time work, short-term contracts, or even taking a step down the career ladder in order to work your way up to a new position.

Problem 9. 'Most of the jobs I've done have been very much the same'

Concentrate on your key skills and achievements and simply summarise your actual career history.

Example

Career profile
A smart, efficient sales consultant and confident in-store demonstrator, experienced in a number of sales environments including TV and video, white goods, and home furnishings.

Key skills
- Customer care
- Cash handling and security
- Stock control, including operating computerised stock control system

- Financial administration, including credit agreements, customer accounts, credit/debit notes, and bank reconciliations
- Clerical administration, including sales reports and customer correspondence

Key achievements

- Organised and managed Sandlands stand at this year's Home Electric Exhibition
- Used computerised stock control system to track and analyse stock movement between five branches
- Organised daily bank deposits of cash and credit card takings
- Member of team winning 'Contact '03' award

Employment record

2005–present	Sandlands Sales and Marketing **Sales Demonstrator**
2002–2005	TV Ten TV & Video Rentals **Sales Consultant**
2000–2002	Whittaker Furnishings **Sales Consultant**

Problem 10. 'I know I'm right for the job, but how can I get that across?'

Special jobs deserve special preparation. When you find a job that you know is just what you're looking for, take extra time and trouble to prepare a CV specifically for that vacancy, using the skills and qualities listed in the job advertisement or job description. Carefully match your own qualifications and experience with the employer's needs.

Chapter 3 has more information about doing this.

Problem 11. 'I'm over-qualified for the job I want'

Emphasise the relevant *practical* skills and experience that you have for the job. Focus attention on your Key strengths and Key skills sections, and choose the skills that fit the job you are applying for. 'Excess' qualifications can be discreetly mentioned in the education section. Highlight, instead, any relevant on-the-job training you have had.

Problem 12. 'I don't have many qualifications'

Concentrate on what you do have. Emphasise your practical skills and experience; these are often more valuable to an employer than theoretical knowledge anyway.

If your lack of qualifications is becoming a serious handicap to your progress, consider applying for further training. This can, increasingly, be undertaken in the workplace without the need to go back to full-time education for two or three years. You may also find that your existing experience can be counted towards a qualification.

Example

Key skills
Customer care

- Receive and seat customers
- Take orders from customers and liaise with the kitchen
- Handle customer enquiries and complaints efficiently

Service

- Provide both à la carte and table d'hôte style service
- Perform silver service and French style food service
- Set tables for meals of up to eight courses

- Serve wine and other beverages
- Clear tables systematically

Key achievements

- Provided silver service at city centre four-star hotel, serving up to 600 people daily at breakfast, lunch and dinner
- Performed waitress service and bar service at major functions
- Served all types and levels of customers efficiently, pleasantly and courteously

Problem 13. 'I'm over 50'

Make sure your CV clearly states your experience and successful track record – these things tend to come only with maturity – and stringently edit your early career history.

This subject is covered more fully in Chapter 8.

Problem 14. 'I'm under 25'

You may be lacking experience. Make full use of any experience you do have, and highlight any skills you may have from school or college, even if you haven't had the opportunity to use them in a work setting.

This subject is covered more fully in Chapter 6.

Problem 15. 'I'm returning to work after bringing up children'

Stress your capabilities, qualities and experience. Highlight any skills you have gained in voluntary positions in the home, school, or in the community, as well as any training or re-training you may be doing in preparation for your return to work.

This subject is covered more fully in Chapter 7.

Problem 16. 'I'm applying for two different types of jobs'

If you're applying for different types of job requiring different abilities and qualities, you will need to have two different CVs, each with a different emphasis.

The following two CVs have been prepared for the same person, the first concentrating on training experience and the second concentrating on sales experience:

Guy Owen

33 Holly Court
Prince's Road
Leeds LS5 2AS

Telephone: 0000 000 0000
e-mail: gowen@anyisp.uk

Career profile

A skilled trainer with over 12 years' experience in training and allied fields. Currently undertaking a wide range of consultative training initiatives in both the private and public sector. Also responsible for the effective coordination of professional services within the company.

Key strengths

The ability to analyse individual training needs: consistently achieved and exceeded training targets by working with trainees as individuals and assessing their specific needs rather than delivering a 'one-size-fits-all' package.

Excellent presentation and communication skills: awarded the Technical Training prize two years running in recognition of my presentation and communication skills.

Training experience

- Successfully trained and licensed a sales force of 50 within three months
- Designed and implemented a new monitoring and assessment system
- Established management training for Branch Sales Managers
- Consistently achieved sales training targets
- Devised and wrote training manuals
- Awarded Technical Training Prize 2006 and 2007

Career summary

2005–present	Training Consultant	ICS Training
2002–2005	Area Sales Manager	Ellenbach Assurance
1998–2002	Head of Sales Training	Mutual Assurance Financiers
1993–1998	Sales Manager	Bradford-Bond Brokerage
1990–1993	Sales Associate	Crown Corporate Investments

Education and training

1998	ASA Associates	Certificate in Training
1988–1990	South Bradley College	HNC Business Studies

Member of the Life Assurance Association

Personal

Date of birth: 17 November 1970

Full, clean UK driving licence

References available on request

Guy Owen

33 Holly Court
Prince's Road
Leeds LS5 2AS

Telephone: 0000 000 0000
e-mail: gowen@anyisp.uk

Career profile

A Senior Sales Executive with a background in sales management, specific experience of business-to-business negotiations and a proven track record in business systems, office supplies and business machines.

Key strengths

A solid background in sales: 15 years' experience of sales and sales training up to Area Sales Manager level and a personal track record in direct selling with a client base exceeding 600 in five years.

Solution selling/consultative approach: achieved an increase of 20 per cent annual profit through rigorously using a consultative approach with clients and trained sales staff how to achieve the same results.

Sales experience

- Personal sales track record in direct selling with a client base exceeding 600 in five years
- Increased sales by 20 per cent over preceding year's totals
- Formulated major policy decisions on all stages of sales activities
- Responsible for new product launches
- Achieved competitive advantage through thorough knowledge of the market
- Successfully set up sales training programme

Career summary

2005–present	Training Consultant	ICS Training
2002–2005	Area Sales Manager	Ellenbach Assurance
1998–2002	Head of Sales Training	Mutual Assurance Financiers
1993–1998	Sales Manager	Bradford-Bond Brokerage
1990–1993	Sales Associate	Crown Corporate Investments

Education and training

1988–1990	South Bradley College	HNC Business Studies
1998	ASA Associates	Certificate in Training

Member of the Life Assurance Association

Personal

Date of birth: 17 November 1970

Full, clean UK driving licence

References available on request

Problem 17. 'I've been unemployed for over a year'

As with many of the problems above, the answer is to draw attention to your positive points and give these the major share of your CV, and to cover only briefly those areas where you may be weaker.

Include the skills you have learned through voluntary work or further training during your period of unemployment. In the example below, the job as Finance Administrator was a full-time voluntary position, but attention isn't drawn to this fact.

Example

Key skills

Management

- Managing and motivating five full-time and up to 20 part-time staff in three branches
- Maximising savings, mortgage sales, and introducing customer services including mortgage debt counselling
- Exceeding targets set for insurance, savings and mortgage lending sales
- Representing Mutual Assurance Group on committee of local Chamber of Commerce

Financial administration

- Running purchase order system and budget control
- Preparing month-end accounts and monthly business reports
- Compiling Management Information Reports and preparing claims for Government Agencies
- Organising and administering payment of office and staff expenses

Information technology

- Proficient in using both spreadsheet and word-processing applications:

    Word
    Excel
    Access
    Outlook
    PowerPoint

Career summary

Currently	Information Technology NVQ level 3	Data Training
2005–2006	Finance Administrator	Cosmopolitan Trust
2001–2005	Group Branch Manager	Mutual Assurance Group
1992–2001	Travel Agency Manager	Bond Travel

Problem 18. 'I have two quite different areas of experience'

This is similar to Problem 16. Consider preparing two quite different CVs, each highlighting one of your two main areas of experience, and using them as appropriate.

Problem 19. 'My last job was actually a bit of a step backwards (or sideways)'

With so many organisations changing their structure and, sometimes, even cutting out whole layers of management, this is true for many people these days.

Don't draw attention to it. Put your abilities and achievements in a separate, major, section and just summarise the rest of your employment details.

Example

Key skills

- Providing a Help Desk for software and hardware queries
- Using VMS and RSX operating systems to recover lost data files
- Analysing system performance, identifying problems and establishing their probable origin before taking appropriate action
- Error logging for both software and hardware
- Installation and implementation of communications equipment using X21, KILOSTREAM and MERCURY links
- Daily backup of data records and transfer of these records to off-site storage
- General maintenance of hardware and data wiring

Career summary

2001–present	Programmer	Sunstream Industries
1998–2001	System Controller	Trust Insurance
1994–1998	Senior System Analyst	Ringwood Assurance
1989–1994	Programmer, data storage and retrieval	Various

Problem 20. 'I've only ever had one job'

Make sure you cover the full range of skills you've used in that job, and include any experience gained from outside interests or voluntary work that will usefully expand your abilities.

Example

Career profile

A well-organised, reliable secretary and receptionist with extensive knowledge of good office practice including word processing, desktop publishing, electronic mail systems, spreadsheets and databases.

Key skills

Secretarial

- RSA III Typewriting – current speed 70 wpm
- RSA II Audio-typing – current speed 70 wpm
- RSA II Shorthand – current speed 120 wpm
- Typing all correspondence and reports
- Preparing spreadsheets and maintaining databases
- Arranging, coordinating and minuting all departmental meetings

Reception

- Operating 20-line switchboard
- Directing all incoming calls, and dealing initially with all queries
- Administering incoming and outgoing mail
- Handling all enquiries at reception, including visitors and deliveries

Career history

Link Holdings Ltd
2004 to present
Receptionist
Secretary to Marketing Department

Starting out

Whether you're leaving school, college or university, what do you put in your CV when you're just starting out?

Personal statement

Without a career history to tell them what sort of interests and aptitudes you have, a potential employer can form a clearer picture of you from a well thought out personal statement.

It can be quite useful to know what you feel your positive qualities are, what you see as your main strengths at this early stage, and also an idea of the direction you hope your career will take.

Qualifications

At this stage in your career, Education and training is probably going to be one of the important sections, so cover it fully – especially if you have been doing a college or university course closely related to the sort of work that you want to do.

Achievements

Highlight any special duties or responsibilities you have undertaken at school or college.

Include anything that rounds out the picture of you as a responsible and dependable individual with experience of more than just the classroom or lecture hall. Convince your future employer that you have qualities that will be useful to them in the workplace.

Work experience

A prospective employer will be interested in any work experience you've had. It doesn't matter if your experience is different from the sort of work you are applying for, it will still demonstrate that you are familiar with a working environment. You can show that you appreciate the importance of punctuality, following instructions, being responsible, etc.

Your experience needn't necessarily be in paid employment. Include any voluntary work that you may have done, as well as work placements or work experience courses, especially if they are relevant to the sort of work that you wish to do.

For more ideas about the sort of qualities employers value, see the section on *Desirable qualities* in the Appendix.

Examples of CVs appear on the following pages:

1. **Richard Quinlan** – school leaver with relevant work experience.
2. **Angela Walker** – school leaver with relevant skills and experience.
3. **Pamela Heart** – school leaver without work experience, but with some voluntary work.
4. **Anthony Dickens** – college leaver with some relevant work experience.
5. **Linda Darin** – college leaver with some work experience.
6. **Kevin Clarke** – graduate with excellent work experience.
7. **Yolande Eden** – university graduate with some work experience.

Richard Quinlan

9 Barge's Brook Lane
Upper Tindle
Warwickshire WR3 6VN

Tel: 0000 0000000

Personal profile

School leaver with workplace experience, a good eye for detail and the ability to work well both independently and as part of a team. With a particular interest in retail work, either sales or marketing.

Key strengths

Previous retail experience: part-time and holiday experience at a local newsagent and a soft-furnishings shop has taught me the value of punctuality and of following instructions accurately, and also developed confidence in my ability to relate to customers and to handle everyday problems appropriately.

Enthusiastic, ambitious and dedicated to customer service: while at Drum House Furnishings, I was trained to listen to customers, identify their requirements and recommend products that would best suit their needs, a role that I greatly enjoyed and wish to develop further.

Education

2003–2008 City Park School
GCSEs:
General Science B; Maths C; German B; History B; English language D

Employment

Kay News newsagents
2006–present
Newspaper Distributor

- Sorted deliveries
- Delivered newspapers and magazines reliably
- Handled enquiries and complaints
- Collected cash

Drum House Furnishings
Summer 2008
Sales and Storeroom Assistant

- Served and assisted customers
- Maintained displays
- Took details of customer orders
- Prepared orders for distribution office

Personal details

Date of birth:	1 February 1992
Health:	Non-smoker
Interests:	Acting and stage management. I belong to the local amateur dramatics club and am secretary to the Drama Youth Group.
References:	Available on request

Angela Walker

31 Pollard Way
Marsh Cross
Cambridge CM14 2KL
Tel: 0000 0000000
e-mail: awalker@anyisp.com

Personal profile:

A highly motivated school leaver with experience of office work. Punctual, reliable and willing to learn, with a good basic education and a strong aptitude for organisation and administration.

Key strengths:

Experience of office work: I have been an after-school voluntary assistant in the school office for the past year, supporting the school secretary and helping with all aspects of administration. My summer work experience was also as an office assistant with a firm of estate agents, carrying out routine office procedures.

Computer literate: trained in Microsoft Office with experience of using Word and Excel.

Key skills:

- Keyboard skills – 40 wpm
- Preparing and writing routine correspondence
- Organising and carrying out routine administrative work
  - maintaining records
  - dealing with incoming telephone calls
  - dealing with incoming mail

Work experience:

Summer 2008; Ashbourn & Sedley
Office Assistant

2007–2008; Marsh Cross School Administration Department
Administrative Assistant (part-time/voluntary)

Education:

2001–2008 Marsh Cross School
GCSEs:

- English language
- English literature
- Maths
- French
- History
- Economics

Introduction to Computer Literacy
RSA Stage I Keyboard Skills
RSA Stage I Office Skills

Personal details:

Date of birth: 30 March 1990
Interests: Riding and pony-trekking, reading and cinema
References available on request

Pamela Heart

87 First Road, Impney
Hereford HE15 6TD

Tel: 0000 0000000
e-mail: pshheart@anyisp.com

Personal profile

A friendly, outgoing person. Reliable, conscientious and happy to work both as part of a team and on own initiative.

Key strengths

Good communication skills and a helpful manner: voluntary work with both elderly people and younger children has developed a good range of communication skills as well as the ability to help and support others conscientiously and diplomatically.

IT skills: fully PC literate, including spreadsheets, e-mail, internet and word processing.

Achievements

- Representing school in Athletics and Cross-Country Running
- Participating in City Marathon 2007
- Secretary of Under-18 Squash and Racquet team
- Elected House Captain

Education

2001–2008 Heath House King's School

A levels:

- French C
- History C

Computer skills:

- Word
- Access
- Excel

GCSEs:

French B; History C; Maths C; General Science C; English language D

Voluntary work experience

Working with the elderly

Regularly visited four residents of local sheltered housing to help with shopping and everyday household tasks.

Holiday Playscheme

Coached under-11s in squash, badminton and tennis in groups of four or five during summer and Easter holidays.

Personal details

Date of birth: 20 April 1990
Non-smoker

Anthony Dickens
7 Yelland Avenue
Port Nearsby
Pickering PS12 7HG

Tel: 0000 0000000
e-mail: adickens@anyisp.com

Personal profile

College graduate with BTEC in Business and Finance and work experience in a banking environment.

Key strengths

Self-motivated and hard-working: have arranged all work experience placements on my own initiative and fulfilled all requirements to the highest satisfaction of each employer. Consistently in top 5 per cent of class for college course.

An understanding of the financial environment: have had work experience at three different banks with the opportunity to observe a comprehensive range of financial procedures.

Education and training

2007 to 2008 **BTEC National Diploma in Business and Finance – year 2**
Thorford College

- Administration systems
- Business environment
- Human resources
- Financial planning and control
- Elements of investment
- Innovation and change
- Business statistics
- Personnel, policies and procedures
- Insurance two

2006 to 2007 **BTEC National Diploma in Business and Finance – year 1**
Thorford College

- Principles and practice of insurance
- Elements of banking
- Accounting procedures
- Business Information Technology
- Financial resources
- Physical resources
- Marketing process

Anthony Dickens (cont.)

2005 to 2006	**BTEC First Diploma in Business and Finance** Eastville College of Further Education • Insurance proficiency one • Production • Business Information Technology • Administrative support • People in business • Business resources and procedures • Administrative systems and procedures • Business world

Work history

2007 to present	**Bealsway** Corington **Cashier and Kiosk Assistant** Responsibilities: • Handled large amounts of money • Customer care • Alcohol and cigarette legislation
Work experience	**National Associative Bank** Corington **Lakeland Bank** Corington **Mansfield Bank** Pickering Responsibilities: • Carried out basic office procedures and clerical work, including filing and photocopying. • Observed and assessed departmental procedures including: – Foreign exchange – Mortgage and lending – Pensions – High-risk accounts – Customer services – Processing room

Additional skills	**Computer skills: Microsoft Office** Familiarity with Windows environment, and use of spreadsheets and databases.
Personal	Date of birth: 18 May 1988
Interests	I enjoy riding and swimming, and support my local football and basketball teams. I also enjoy listening to music.
References	Available on request

Linda Darin

34 Southernwood Drive
Hendy Hill
Edgerton
Surrey SR21 9AS

Tel. 00000 000000
e-mail: ldarin@anyisp.com

Personal profile

College graduate with sales and voluntary work experience looking for an entry-level opportunity in travel and tourism that will allow me to make use of my theoretical knowledge while acquiring practical skills.

Key strengths

Good customer relations skills: my experience of working with the public in retail, fundraising and youth work has taught me the value of friendliness, open-mindedness and having a good sense of humour as well as how to communicate effectively at all levels.

Qualification in environmental, tourism or related subject area: I have recently completed a two-year BTEC National Diploma in Travel and Tourism.

Competent IT skills: trained and experienced in using Word, Excel and Outlook Express.

Employment

Hall Dean Markets
2005–2006
Sales Assistant

- Served and assisted customers
- Handled cash
- Dealt with enquiries and complaints

Voluntary work experience

- Raised funds for CCRF (Childhood Cancer Relief Fund)
- Worked with children with learning difficulties

Education and training

2006–2008 Edgerton College
BTEC National Diploma in Travel and Tourism
The course covered all aspects of travel and tourism, including:

- Worldwide travel geography
- Airport operations
- Resort representatives
- Finance
- Travel services

Linda Darin (cont.)

Language Skills:
- Spanish
- Italian
- German
- French

Computer Skills:
- Word
- Access

2000–2006 Edgerton School
GCSEs:
Five including Maths and English
Services to Business
Services to People

Personal details

Date of birth:	19 July 1989
Licence:	Full, clean UK driving licence
Interests:	Member of: Edgerton hockey club Edgerton athletics club Southland athletics club Affiliated to the BSJA (horse riding)
References:	Available on request

Kevin Clarke
16 Whiteside Gardens,
Kesdale
Lincs LN5 7TU

Tel: (0132) 0000000
e-mail: kclarke@unorth.ac.uk

Personal profile

Biological Sciences graduate with first-hand laboratory and administrative experience in an industrial environment and an understanding of the requirements of a commercial organisation. Quick to learn and used to adapting to high pressure and tight deadlines while remaining both good-humoured and accurate.

Work experience

Summer 2008
Dale Chemicals
Laboratory Assistant:

- Responsible for trials of chemical scrubbing techniques
- Administered trial process
- Analysed data and prepared reports accordingly

Summer 2007
Seabright Pharmaceuticals
General Assistant:

- Coordinated administration of full-scale drug trials
- Responsible for data collation requiring 100% accuracy
- Prepared interim reports
- Carried out administrative requirements of the department

Education

2006–2009	University of the North **BSc (Hons) Biological Sciences – 2(ii)**	
1999–2006	Kesdale High School	
	GCSEs	Seven GCSEs including Maths and English
	A levels	Maths, Chemistry, Biology
Computer literacy:	Word Access	
Languages:	Conversational French	

Personal details

Date of birth	15 November 1988
Interests	Reading, swimming, music
References	Available on request

Yolande Eden

77 Terrence Place
Long Common
Cheshire CH15 8SX

Tel: (0000) 0000000
e-mail: yeden@wmu.ac.uk

Career objective: A Computer Science graduate with a keen interest in practical applications and information systems, seeking a career where a background in problem-solving would be an advantage.

Key strengths: **A self-starter with a high level of initiative:** devised and implemented design of final-year project, proposed it to West Midlands NHS and delivered new geographical database currently used by department.

Strong organisation and planning skills: planned and organised comprehensive programme for summer FutureFit project with a team of five, giving local schools hands-on coaching and demonstrations of how technology can improve sports performance.

Fast learner who thrives in a rapidly changing environment: learned to use GI Systems in three weeks in order to undertake final-year project. My interest in robotics and AI attest to my interest in leading-edge, rapidly changing technology.

Education:

2005–2008 **BSc Computer Science**
West Midlands University

Year 3

- **Robotics:**
  concepts
  VAL
  3-D modelling of components
  assembly
  matrices
- **Graphics:**
  2-D and 3-D projection
  transformation matrices
- **Communications:**
  network theory
  protocols
  hardware
- **Database Theory:**
  structure
  storage
  design
- **Formal Logic:**
  trinary
  fuzzy
  temporal
- **Artificial Intelligence:**
  Popll
  expert systems
  Prolog
  theory of neural nets

Final-Year Project:
The Use of Geographical Information Systems. The project was to write a geographical database which, using a GIS package, could plot NHS patient data for the West Midlands. Project included use of OS map data. Package used: Arc-Info under X-Windows on a DEC workstation

Yolande Eden (cont.)

Year 2	• **Computer Science:** database design with SSADM Ad programming micro-electronics formal logic software design methods	• **Maths:** transformation matrices with coordinate systems multiple differentiation integration
Year 1	• **Computer Science:** software management programming methodologies micro-electronics programming in Ada	• **Maths:** graphs and matrices complex equations differential equations integration with trigonometric functions

Key skills:

- **Programming languages:**
  - Ada
  - Pascal
  - Popll
  - Prolog
  - VAL
  - SML
  - C
  - Modula 2
  - Clipper 5
  - ArcInfo
- **Environments:**
  - Sunview
  - X-Windows
  - MS-Windows
  - Apple Mac
  - UNIX
  - MSDOS

Work experience:

Summer 2007 **Tripp Electronics**
Littledean
Administrative Assistant

Summer 2006 **Torrington Newcombe**
Olstead
Clerical Assistant

Summer 2005 **Tripp Electronics**
Littledean
Clerk

Personal:

Date of birth: 19 January 1983
Full, clean UK driving licence

Interests:

I am an active member of the University Irish Folk Club and enjoy music, listening and performing, and dancing. I also enjoy cycling and swimming.

7

Starting again

At some time in your life, you may find yourself re-entering the job market after a break. This can be for a number of reasons: bringing up a family, taking time out for travel or voluntary work, or redundancy or unemployment.

Don't apologise for your career break. Gaps in employment, for whatever reason, are a fact of life and should be handled positively and assertively.

Emphasise your relevant experience and concentrate on your skills and qualities. Draw attention to what you have done, rather than what you haven't.

Career profile

You may be returning to a different type of job from the one that you used to do. If so, make use of the Career profile at the top of the page to connect the three parts of your working life: your previous employment, your experience during the break, and your future direction.

Key skills

Highlight your key skills, achievements or qualifications. Include any gained through voluntary or part-time work during your career break. Include, too, qualifications and skills gained through education or training, and mention any ways in which you have kept abreast of developments in your trade or profession.

You might like to add positive ways in which you have changed: increased maturity, for example, or more responsibility, confidence, understanding, new skills, insight, etc.

Career history

What have you done during your break?

Depending on how long you have been out of employment, things may have changed a lot since you last worked. Employers sometimes worry about returners being out of date with what's happening in the industry. They may wonder if you will be willing to adapt to new ways of doing things, or if you will stick to the ways that you already know.

Point out how you have kept up your skills, and mention anything that you have done to improve or update them. Any training you have done during this time will be a useful indicator of your interest and motivation. It's not a bad idea, in any case, to go back to the workplace better qualified than when you left it.

Include all the work experience you have had during your career break, including voluntary work, part-time work, special responsibilities and duties, etc. Even if it was unpaid, an employer will still be interested in what you have done recently.

Examples of CVs appear on the following pages:

1. **Janet Sandiman** – returning after child-care, looking for a career change after training.

2. **Ananda Vires** – returning after child-care, voluntary work experience.
3. **Daniel Guys** – returning to full-time work after extensive travelling.
4. **Edward Kingsman** – returning after redundancy with further training and related voluntary work.
5. **Diane Walker** – returning after redundancy with updated training.

JANET SANDIMAN
14 Eastover Common, Oxhill
Avon AV20 4CP

Tel: 0000 0000000
e-mail: jmnsandiman@anyisp.com

Career objective

A mature and responsible individual with counselling skills and broad experience of nursing and caring for others, now looking for the opportunity to work with clients and assist them to explore their concerns, focus on underlying issues, and consider options towards setting and achieving goals.

Key strengths

Experience of building a long-term relationship with clients: AEB/CAC training is practical-skills based and includes experience of building client relationships both short (brief therapy) and long term.

Ability to relate to people of different backgrounds: as a nurse, required to deal tactfully, sympathetically and effectively with people of all ages and backgrounds and help them to feel as comfortable as possible in a strange and often intimidating environment.

Key skills

- Encouraging and motivating others
- Providing counselling support for trauma and bereavement
- Preparing others for, and supporting them through, life changes
- An understanding of women's health issues
- Computer literate

Key qualifications

- State Enrolled Nurse
- Certificate of Counselling Theory AEB/CAC
- Certificate of Counselling Practice AEB/CAC
- Open Access vocational training in:
  - Post-Trauma Stress and Critical Incident Debriefing
  - Primary Health Care Counselling
  - Managing Short-Term Counselling Work within Primary Care
  - Women and Mental Health

Career history

2002–present
Responsible for the full-time care of my two children, now at school, while also undergoing training as a counsellor.

1998–2002
Leigh House Hospital

State Enrolled Nurse

Responsible for medical and surgical patients:

- Prepared patients physically and mentally for surgery
- Provided patient care post-surgery

Janet Sandiman (cont.)

- Supported and counselled relatives of terminal patients
- Assisted on ward rounds
- Updated patient records
- Administered drugs
- Dealt with enquiries from patients and their families

1996–1998
Eastern Hospital
State Enrolled Nurse
Responsible for day-to-day working in out-patients department:

- Supported patients and provided patient care
- Assisted with routine procedures
- Dealt with enquiries from patients and their families
- Prepared working areas
- Compiled patient records

Education and training

2003–2005 Westbrook College of Further Education
Certificate of Counselling Theory AEB/CAC
Certificate of Counselling Practice AEB/CAC

2004–2007 Oxhill Community College
Open Access vocational courses:

- Post-Trauma Stress and Critical Incident Debriefing
- Primary Health Care Counselling
- Managing Short-Term Counselling Work within Primary Care
- Women and Mental Health

1992–1994 Langport Hospital
Student Nurse for State Enrolled Nurse

1987–1992 St Lawrence School for Girls
Six GCSEs, including Maths, English, Chemistry and Biology

Personal details

Date of birth:	9 July 1978
Licence:	Full, clean UK driving licence, own car
Interests:	Computers, education, active member of the Oxhill community volunteers group
References:	Available on request

Ananda Vires
2 Gorstan Mead, Matley
North Yorkshire NY19 7DC
Tel: 0000 0000000

Career profile:

A reliable, conscientious and efficient computer-literate administrator with good secretarial and organisational skills. Proficient at working both on own initiative and as part of a team.

Key strengths:

Efficient: as secretary of the Residents Association, required to turn correspondence and reports around in the shortest time possible and keep all interested parties informed and up to date. Responsible for planning meetings, ensuring venues are booked, members and guests notified, relevant paperwork available and any mishaps dealt with. Voted in as secretary three years running and given special vote of thanks for excellent work.

Reliable: have proved totally dependable as association secretary, as a working-party member, member of several committees and Tenants' Forum representative, giving 100 per cent commitment to any role I take on.

Articulate: required to liaise with the Housing Office and to represent the Association at meetings of the Tenants' Forum and at special interest groups.

Key skills:

- Secretarial, including word-processing
  - Word for Windows
  - Excel
  - Microsoft Outlook
- Excellent telephone manner
- Resourceful, reliable team member

Career history:

Matley North End Residents Association
2004–ongoing
Secretary
Organised and administered voluntary Tenants' Association:

- Organised monthly meetings and annual general meetings
- Wrote, typed and circulated minutes
- Dealt with correspondence
- Liaised with Housing Office
- Drafted reports on specific issues as member of various working parties
- Represented Association at meetings of other organisations, the Tenants' Forum and special interest groups

2000–present
During this period I have also been caring for my children full-time.

Ananda Vires (cont.)

Benn, Hodge and Keen
1995–2000
Secretary
Responsible for secretarial support to department:

- Typed reports and correspondence
- Organised appointments and arranged meetings
- Minuted all departmental meetings
- Responded to telephone enquiries and requests
- Coordinated department work schedule.

Coburg & Partners
1990–1995
Secretary/clerk
Organised and carried out routine office administration, maintained records and files, dealt with incoming mail, prepared routine correspondence

---

Education:

Community Open College
2007–2008
Computer Literacy (CLAIT) Stages I & II
Introduction to Information Technology
RSA Stage I Office Skills

Holm Place School
1983–1991
GCSEs:
Seven including Maths and English
A levels:

- English language
- English literature
- French

Personal details:

Date of birth: 10 March 1972
Interests: Badminton, swimming
Car owner/driver with full, clean UK licence
References available on request

Daniel Guys
68 St John's Road, Adrington
East Sussex SX4 2JN

Tel: 0000 0000000

Career profile:

A graduate with first-rate language skills gained through both formal study and extensive travel, as well as teaching English as a Foreign Language in Europe, seeking a position that will allow me to use my experience and abilities to good effect in a forward-thinking, Europe-orientated organisation.

Key strengths:

European focused, with knowledge of at least one European language: have lived and worked in France, Spain and Sweden, interacting with local and business communities. French and Spanish speaking.

Drive and initiative: devised and delivered property-focused Business English course for small businesses; devised suitable material for student language groups; self-funded all travel through finding work or sponsorship.

Key skills:

Languages:

- Fluent written and spoken French
  - Conversational
  - Business
  - Literary
- Excellent Business and Conversational Spanish

Tuition:

- Teaching Business English to Spanish business people in on-site training programmes
- Teaching Adult Education classes in France
- Teaching student groups in Swedish summer school

Other:

- Computer literate, including word-processing packages and spreadsheets
- Experienced in meeting deadlines, dealing with clients, office procedures, and compiling records

Work experience:

Travelling in Africa, Asia and Europe
2004–2008
Teacher of English as a Foreign Language

Responsible for teaching English to a variety of students:

- Delivered teaching programmes to several professional companies
- Taught Business English at all levels from students to company directors
- Devised and taught mixed-ability adult evening class

Daniel Guys (cont.)

- Encouraged and motivated students
- Organised leisure activities for multilingual groups of students at residential summer school

Torrington Ellis Ltd
2002–2004
Claims Supervisor
Initially employed as a graduate clerk/trainee, I was promoted to Claims Supervisor:

- Dealt with telephone enquiries and correspondence
- Processed claims
- Issued cheques
- Ensured deadlines were kept
- Prepared claims

Education:

South East College
2005
RSA Certificate
Teaching English as a Foreign Language

University of East Midlands
1999–2003
BA Hons 2:1
French Language and Literature

Fairchurch Secondary School
1992–1999
GCSEs:
Seven including Maths and English

A levels:

- English literature
- French
- History

Personal details:

Date of birth: 10 August 1981
Interests: Foreign cinema, food and cookery, hill-walking
Health: Non-smoker
Prepared to relocate
References available on request

Edward Kingsman
The Firs
8 Langport Road
Coveringham
Lincoln
LN12 2JH

Tel: 0000 0000000
e-mail: ekingsman@anyisp.com

Career profile

A skilled engineer with both practical and managerial skills, gained through many years' experience of supervising staff including apprentices and trainees. An outgoing, down-to-earth person who enjoys being involved with whatever is going on, and has encountered and solved many problems with both machines and people.

Key skills

- Managing staff in a high-turnover production environment
- Providing a first-rate engineering service to internal and external customers
- Project management and budget preparation
- Training and motivating staff
- Computer literate

Career history

JMF Training Consortium
2003–present
Training Supervisor
Trained Community Project volunteers in basic engineering skills for a variety of projects including environmental and conservation work.

G&T Tower Ltd
2000–2003
Industrial Engineer
Responsible for all industrial engineering services at factory and divisional level. Monitored, coordinated and delivered production engineering service with particular emphasis on product costing, value engineering, pre-production engineering and methods improvement. Provided work measurement facilities and maintained bonus scheme.

APT Engineering Ltd
1993–2000
Director/Partner
Planned, organised and implemented all aspects of running a small engineering company.

Edward Kingsman (cont.)

Pearl Valves Ltd
1988–1993
Foreman Supervisor
Managed day-to-day control of production lines on a two-shift system. Supervised leading hands, setters and operatives, production planning, quality assurance, coordination of tools and materials and bonus scheme administration. Promoted to position after joining company in 1981.

Education and training

2008 CRO Training Services
City & Guilds Training for Trainers Certificate

2006 Open University
The Effective Manager

1986–1988 Keyfield College
City & Guilds Certificate in Mechanical Engineering

North East College
Supplementary certificates:

- Toolroom Practices
- Inspection and Quality Assurances
- Health and Safety Planning

In-work training
Internal and external courses:

- Accountancy Part I & II
- Team management skills
- Negotiation skills
- Computer Smartware II
- Spreadsheets
- Word-processing

Personal details

Date of birth:	9 March 1968
Licence:	Full, clean UK driving licence, advanced motorist's certificate
Interests:	Computers and computing, conservation (I am a member of the local environmental and conservation group), current affairs, swimming.
References:	Available on request

DIANE WALKER
83 Draycot Place,
Eastley, Surrey SR1 2AA

Telephone: 0000 0000000

Career profile

An experienced administrator and office manager with an extensive knowledge of business practices especially in accounting, bookkeeping, and inventory control.

Key strengths

Excellent IT and administrative skills: currently completing NVQ level 3 course to upgrade administrative and office management skills as well as IT skills. Experienced user of Microsoft Office and Windows XP across a range of functions.

Attention to detail: in my last position, I was responsible for administration of all purchase and inventory documentation and records, requiring a high degree of organisation and attention to detail. Previously I was responsible for analysing and rectifying errors in customer' accounts, which also required an excellent eye for detail.

Ability to supervise staff: have supervised a total of eight staff in a busy retail environment and have also been trained to NVQ level 3 in Supervision.

Key skills

- Supervising staff
- Implementing standard procedures accurately
- Prioritising workload
- Analysing and rectifying errors
- Conversational French
- Computer skills:
  - Word
  - Excel
  - Access

Career history

2007–present	Eastley Training Centre **NVQ level 3 Clerical Skills Course** Administration and Supervision. Advanced course to update and expand office management skills
1998–2006	Friends Assurance Association **Office Administrator** Responsible for all documentation and records. Also dealt with queries, and the organisation of data within the department
1994–1998	Keyline Retail **Section Manager** Supervised staff and attended to customers in busy city centre store. Responsible for daily administration of section including stock control, turnover, and complaints

Diane Walker (cont.)

1990–1994	Scottish Finance Co. **Office Administrator** Analysed and rectified accounting errors in customer accounts
1987–1990	United Insurance Ltd **Office Administrator** Carried out administrative work of department including invoicing and ordering. Processed payroll and coordinated work schedules

Education and training

2007–present	Eastley Training Centre NVQ level 3 Clerical Skills Course concentrating on administration and supervision. This advanced course updates and expands my current office management skills, and also covers Information Technology.
1987–1988	Oldbarrow College of Further Education College Secretarial Diploma
1982–1987	Impney Court School GCSEs: seven, including Maths and English A levels: French, English, Economics

Personal details

Date of birth:	12 December 1969
Health:	Non-smoker
Driving:	Full, clean UK licence
Interests:	I work as a dresser for charity fashion shows on a freelance basis at evenings and weekends. This involves being able to keep to a tight timetable, work quickly and accurately, and remain cool, calm and collected under extreme pressure.
References:	Available on request

Keeping going

There is now anti-age discrimination law and employers' attitudes *are* changing, but if you are 45 or over, you may wonder how to present yourself in the best light so as to maximise your employment and promotion chances.

Concentrate on the positives. Employers perceive older workers as stable and reliable, mature in their approach, and with good interpersonal skills. Many young people have these qualities too, of course. But one thing older people can offer that younger people may not be able to is experience.

How can you emphasise your experience without filling your CV with a long list of previous jobs?

Career profile

Summarise your career path in the Career profile at the top of your CV. This can speak more fully and persuasively for you than a list of job titles in your Career history section.

Key experience

Rather than a Key skills or Qualifications section, consider including a Key experience section instead. This will clearly emphasise what could be one of your strongest selling points.

Achievements

Demonstrate that your experience brings results and that you have the track record to prove it. Your key achievements can be combined with your key experience, put in a separate section, or clearly listed under your Career history.

Career history

Concentrate on your most recent jobs and edit the rest ruthlessly. For early work, consider simply listing jobs and job titles, and/or grouping jobs together under the heading 'Various'.

Personal details

There is nothing to say you *must* include your date of birth on your CV, and it is up to you whether you include it or not.

However, by the time a reader reaches this final section, they should have formed a positive impression of you that will persuade them to consider your application whatever your age.

Examples of CVs appear on the following pages:

1. **Valerie David** – continuing as a project manager.
2. **Dominic Hoy** – continuing as an electrical engineer.
3. **Alan Bevan** – continuing voluntary work after retirement.

VALERIE DAVID
17 Three Elms Field
Garby
Stourling HU21 5GN
Tel: 0000 0000000 (home)
0000 0000000 (mobile)

Career profile

A highly trained, confident and effective **project manager** with significant experience in a broad range of construction, manufacturing and industrial projects and proven skills in exploring, designing and implementing solutions and the management of change.

Key strengths

Initiative: my current role as project manager requires highly developed problem-solving skills and the ability to respond to crises swiftly and effectively.

Excellent communication skills: it is essential to liaise effectively with management, technical staff and contractors and to consult with all those actively involved in the project to understand comprehensive user-needs and to give information in a way it can be understood and assimilated.

Key experience

- Ten years' experience in project management working in a wide range of environments
- Knowledge of health and safety and employment legislation and practice
- An understanding of staff motivation and training
- A clear commitment to excellence
- An established track record in effective solutions

Career history

Bell & Dutton Consultants
1998 to present

Project Manager

Actively managed a number of projects, including:

Dann Environmental Ltd
Project – Resources and Traffic
Managed traffic flow and resources during development of existing sites and establishment of new 20-acre industrial site:

- Liaised with external consultants
- Gathered, verified and analysed traffic flow data
- Maintained information flow between departments

Revised site layout and traffic handling patterns, resulting in:

- Expansion and full use of most effective areas
- Elimination of single deliveries in favour of multiple stock drops
- Improved vehicle safety

Whitby Transport Group
Project – Storage and Stock Handling
Developed and improved stock storage and handling system:

- Researched safety regulations
- Devised simplified visual verification system
- Designed and oversaw implementation of new system

Valerie David (cont.)

Devised and implemented introduction of new storage systems, resulting in:

- Improved stock handling and rotation
- Reduced stock holding
- Safer working practices
- Improved storage facility of flammable and explosive material

The Industrial Training Group Ltd
1990 to 1998

Training Manager

Managed and administered training projects for agency serving up to 50 local engineering companies:

- Researched opportunities for improvement in services to clients
- Determined supervisory management training needs

Produced comprehensive analysis of training opportunities, skills gaps and information management systems, resulting in:

- Fully costed training scheme and syllabus
- Effective development and expansion of training group

Various
Pre-1990

Management and administrative

A range of managerial and administrative positions for various companies. Responsibilities and achievements over this period include:

- Ensured safe operation of chemical plant during site development
- Increased production turnover of organics at agrochemical company
- Served on safety and work practices committee
- Contributed to operations manual
- Instituted new management control and information systems

Education and training

MBA
Southern School of Business

Diploma in Supervisory Management
Diploma in Operations Management
Cork West College

Computer skills:

- CLAIT Certificate in computer literacy
- Word
- Excel
- Outlook
- PowerPoint

Personal details

Date of birth:	8 September 1958
Interests:	Environmental issues
	Wildlife and wildlife photography
Health:	Non-smoker

Car owner/driver with full, clean UK licence

Dominic Hoy
4 Clements Avenue
High Cross
Berkshire
BK17 5LM

Tel: 0000 0000000
e-mail: ddmhoy@anyisp.com

Career profile

A skilled and experienced electrical engineer, expert in all aspects of installation, servicing and repair, together with an understanding of staff supervision and management gained in a variety of environments.

Key skills and experience

- Over 10 years' experience in electrical engineering
- Knowledge of installing, servicing and repairing electro-mechanical and electronic equipment
- An understanding of precision instrumentation
- An established track record in staff supervision
- A clear commitment to high standards

Career history

2000 to present
Caversham Electrical Engineering
Section Supervisor
Electrical Fitter
Worked in measurement division and repair shop:

- Repaired electronic and electro-mechanical equipment
- Performed or verified precision instrument calibration
- Supervised, administered and co-ordinated 10 full-time and 3 part-time staff
- Planned work schedules
- Maintained work-sheet records
- Oversaw apprentice training
- Ensured excellent standard of department maintained
- Promoted to Supervisor in 2003

Dominic Hoy (cont.)

1989 to 2000
Scouts Engineering
Electrical Maintenance Engineer
Worked in maintenance shop and with overhead cranes and hoists:

- Repaired high-speed machine tools
- Serviced overhead equipment
- Overhauled and maintained equipment
- Maintained control equipment
- Performed general electrical maintenance on the site
- Maintained high standards within tight deadlines

Prior to 1989
Various
Electrical Engineer
Responsible for electrical engineering and maintenance in a variety of situations including early experience with electronics and some communications.

Completed apprenticeship in electrical engineering with Abbott Engineering.

Education and training

City & Guilds
Electrical Engineering

Specialist training courses:

- Control equipment for high-speed tools
- Precision instrument calibration and maintenance

Personal details

Date of birth: 16 May 1963

Interests: Sailing
Studying for Coastal Navigation Certificate
Swimming

Health: Non-smoker

Car owner/driver with full, clean UK licence

References available on request

Alan Bevan

50 April Way, Whitpool
Kent KT3 6ZP

Tel: 0000 0000000 (mobile)

Career objective

Human resources officer with a fundamental interest in workplace equality together with practical experience of helping young people and those with physical disabilities into rewarding and satisfying employment. Keen to continue using these skills and expertise for the benefit of the community.

Key strengths

Organised: currently responsible for HR function for 700 staff across three sites requiring the highest degree of organisation.

A broad range of personnel skills: 12 years' experience overall HR function including employment law, union practice, training and development, psychometric testing, and performance evaluation systems.

Flexible and adaptable: also created and currently administer voluntary career advice service for people with handicaps. Instrumental in all aspects of the service together with a volunteer staff of seven.

Key skills and experience

- Considerable experience in all aspects of human resource assessment and development
- Highly evolved skills in personnel management
- Extensive contacts within training agencies, Training and Enterprise Councils, and employers
- Qualified and experienced in the use of psychometric and aptitude testing
- Experienced in devising, delivering and assessing training courses
- Thorough knowledge of employment law

Career history

2001 to present
Perryman Goldley
Human Resources Manager

- Overall personnel function for office and general staff
- Developed personnel policies and procedures for financial group
- Improved effectiveness of human resource development strategies
- Managed introduction of performance evaluation system

Life Line
2007 to present
Voluntary helper

- Set up and administered career advice and job search service for young people with physical handicaps

Alan Bevan (cont.)

- Represented Life Line at the Business Network Forum to promote equality in the workplace
- Liaised with local TEC and FEFC for education and training opportunities and funding

Terrence Parnell Co Ltd
1990 to 2001
Personnel Officer

- Complete personnel function for Head Office and Southern Region Staff
- Administered records, pay and contractual documents
- Promoted from assistant personnel officer in 1989

Fleet Industrial
1980 to 1990
Personnel Assistant
Clerical Officer
Clerical Assistant

Previous clerical and administrative experience gained in a variety of roles between leaving Fieldhouse College and joining Fleet Industrial.

Education and training

Fellow of the Institute of Personnel and Development

Diploma in Personnel Management
Lincoln Business School

Diploma in Education
Fieldhouse College

Work-related training:
- Psychometric testing
- Aptitude testing
- Assessment skills
- Careers guidance and counselling

Personal details

Date of birth	14 March 1960
Interests	Photography Fell-walking – active member and secretary of Sindon Lake Walkers' Club

Car owner/driver with full, clean UK licence

References available on request

9

CVs for practical jobs

Organisations depend on trustworthy people doing practical jobs reliably. If jobs such as building maintenance, security, deliveries and the like are not done accurately, effectively and efficiently, other employees will be prevented from carrying out their own work.

A prospective employer reading your CV wants to know that you'll be able to do the job competently and skilfully. Demonstrate clearly that you know what needs to be done and that you know how to do it.

The most important areas to emphasise are your past experience, along with any recognised training you have in this particular skill. These will be a good indication of your ability to perform well in the future.

The key qualities needed for most practical jobs are:

- knowledge and hands-on experience of the job;
- these days, usually, proof of adequate training such as NVQ or City & Guilds qualifications;
- competence and reliability;
- self-reliance *as well as* the ability to follow instructions accurately;
- flexibility.

What will help to get these points across?

Career profile

An idea of the work you have done in the past, the amount of experience you have had, and your current position, will all be useful information to a potential employer.

If you have personal qualities that are useful in your job, such as patience or confidence in dealing with the public, mention these as well.

Key skills

You may need specific qualifications for some types of practical work – an HGV licence for some sorts of driving, or a Hygiene Certificate for catering jobs. If you have relevant qualifications, put them in this section where they can be clearly seen.

Concentrate too on the practical skills that you need for your job and which have proved useful in the past. Make it clear that you understand what the job requires.

Career history

Emphasise the experience you have gained in each job, and the skills you have developed through doing it. Mention any specific responsibilities you have had.

The examples on the following pages show an outline CV, and CVs that make use of some or all of the above points. Mary Weber's CV is preceded by the job ad it was written for.

1. **Outline CV.**
2. **Mary Weber** – Chef.
3. **Robert Morgan** – Driver.
4. **Diane Donnelly** – Dental hygienist.
5. **Peter Ruckerby** – Maintenance worker.
6. **Paul Colston** – Warehouse supervisor.

(**Your Name** in large, bold type)
(Your full address)

____

____

____

(Postcode)

(Telephone number, including area code)

(e-mail address)

Career profile

(A brief, businesslike description of yourself)

(Skills)

(Experience)

(Personal strengths)

Key strengths

(Your skills, experience and personal qualities that most closely match the job requirements

Key skills

- (The main skills you have got)
- (Particularly those appropriate to the job you are applying for)
- __________
- __________
- __________

Career history

(**Name of company**, usually starting with the most recent)

(Dates you worked there)

(Job title)

(Brief description of what you did)

____

(Brief description of what you achieved in this position)

- __________
- __________
- __________

(**Name of company**, usually starting with the most recent)

(Dates you worked there)

(Job title)

(Brief description of what you did)

____

(Brief description of what you achieved in this position)

- __________
- __________

Name (cont.)

(**Name of company**, usually starting with the most recent)

(Dates you worked there)

(Job title)

(Brief description of what you did. Jobs you did some years ago require less detail than do your more recent ones)

Education and training

(Starting with the highest, most recent OR most relevant qualification)

(**Name of school, college, or university**)

(Dates you attended)

(The qualification you achieved)
(You could include brief details of what was covered in the course, especially if recently qualified)

-
-
-

(**Name of school, college, or university**)

(Dates you attended)

(The qualification you achieved)

(**Name of school, college, or university**)

(Dates you attended)

(The qualification you achieved)

(Don't go back further than your senior or secondary school)

(**Professional training**)

(Details of any professional training undertaken at work)

- (Qualification or skill achieved)
-
-
-

Personal details

(Date of birth)

(Driving licence)

(Married or single – only if relevant)

(Nationality – only if relevant)

(Interests and activities. Brief details)

(References – usually 'available on request')

Spa Chef

Copperhill Health Spa has an opening for an experienced chef. Working as part of the Catering team and reporting to the Facilities Manager, you will be responsible for providing a high standard of meals and service to meet the nutritional needs of residents, visitors and Spa staff.

You will be expected to accept full responsibility for all catering services and kitchen management in the absence of the Facility Manager.

A recognised catering/food safety qualification such as NVQ Level 3 or City & Guilds equivalent is required.

This is a demanding role that requires excellent organisational skills and a proven ability to multi-task, with experience of working in a medium to large kitchen/restaurant and customer-focused environment; familiarity with ordering and stock control would be an advantage. If you have catering experience within a care environment, so much the better.

If you feel you are the person we are looking for, please sent your CV to Beth Rogers at ____________________.

Turn to the next page to see how Mary Weber has used information in this job ad to give her CV focus and relevance by customising her Career profile and Key strengths sections.

Mary Weber
16 Woodland Road, Little Hadby
Norfolk NF14 9MT
Tel: 00000 000000

Career profile:

Thoroughly trained chef with experience in both the care environment and commercial catering and an understanding of a variety of requirements from stringent nutritional needs to exceptional standards of preparation and presentation.

Key strengths:

Experienced: City & Guilds qualified with seven years' experience in catering, including a hospital environment and a high-quality private catering company.

Excellent organisation and multi-tasking skills: at present working in a high-volume, high-pressure environment preparing meals to exacting standards requiring a high degree of organisation. Working as part of a team requiring flexibility, adaptability and the ability to multi-task in order to keep the kitchen running smoothly and efficiently under all circumstances.

Ordering, stock control and kitchen management experience: currently supervise daily food preparation by a team of 12 including 3 junior assistants. Responsible for maintaining stock control sheets and stock ordering sheets, an exacting task in such a high-volume environment.

Key skills:

- City & Guilds 706 1 & 2
- Intermediate Food Hygiene Certificate
- Thorough understanding of health and safety regulations
- Knowledge of chilled meals production
- Experience of therapeutic diet preparation

Career history:

2006–present
St Edwards District Health Care Trust
Chef
Worked as member of team providing full meals service within central kitchen preparation unit for large hospital trust producing 5,000 meals a day:

- Prepared meals for consumption within the Trust and other hospitals and day centres

Mary Weber (cont.)

- Supervised routine food preparation
- Prepared food with regard to special dietary requirements such as diabetic, low salt, low fat, gluten free, etc
- Undertook preparation of food for chilling and distribution
- Packed and presented food effectively and attractively

2000 to 2006
SSB Resources South East
Chef
Assistant Chef
Provided high-quality catering service to staff and visitors for a number of large commercial clients, working both on own initiative and as part of a team:

- Prepared breakfast and lunch for up to 2,500 people per day
- Undertook pastry and some confectionery work
- Delivered hospitality service requiring exceptionally high standards of preparation and presentation

1998 to 2000
Five Mile Hill School
Assistant Canteen Cook
Assisted preparation of lunchtime meals service for 1,750 children and staff including menu choices and food prepared to special requirements

---

Education and training:

Norfolk City College (day release)

- City & Guilds 706 Cookery For The Catering Industry Part II
- Intermediate Food Hygiene Certificate

South Eastern College of Technology

- City & Guilds 706 Cookery For The Catering Industry Part I

St Edwards and District Secondary School

- Six GCSEs, including English and Maths

Personal details:

Date of birth: 21 February 1978
Health: Non-smoker
Interests: All aspects of conservation – National Trust
World Wide Fund for Nature
RSPB

References available on request

Robert Morgan
Flat 1, Riverside Court
Chiderton
Northumberland NB14 5FL

Tel: 0000 0000000

Career profile:

A capable, professional delivery and PCV driver, with an excellent driving record and experience of organising own round. Fully responsible for planning and delivery on own route, as well as proficient at dealing with the public in a confident and friendly manner.

Key strengths:

Energetic, enthusiastic and reliable: I am proud of my 100 per cent record of punctuality and attendance in my current job. I am required to transport fragile technical products and confidential waste reliably, and have done so to the complete satisfaction of both clients and management. I'm sure colleagues and supervisors would agree that I am always happy to 'go the extra mile'.

Team player: currently required to organise daily deliveries and weekly timetable between a team of three drivers, which requires planning and negotiation to achieve the most efficient schedule for all concerned. Worked very much as part of the Care Team as a PST driver to give the best possible service to patients.

Multi-drop experience: currently make up to 15 drops a day, with responsibility for route planning and loading accordingly.

Key skills:

- Clean current UK driving licence
- PCV licence
- Thorough knowledge of the North East area
- Passenger carrying and multi-drop experience
- Able to plan and prioritise schedules and routes as well as work to instruction
- Smart appearance
- Punctual, healthy, reliable

Career history:

2002 to present
Bourne & Thomas Ltd
Delivery Driver

- Planned and carried out multi-drop deliveries
- Collected confidential waste safely

Robert Morgan (cont.)

- Transported technical products securely and competently
- Planned and organised daily and weekly schedules in agreement with team of drivers
- Maintained schedules and timetables punctually and reliably

1998–2002
NE Central Healthcare Trust
Patient Services Transport Driver

- Provided driver support for Ring and Ride scheme
- Covered two district hospital outpatient departments, three clinics and three day centres
- Arranged most efficient patient pick-up routes in association with Assistant Transport Controller
- Collected outpatients from home and took to destination
- Assisted special needs patients on and off vehicle

1995 to 1998
Pescod Foods Ltd
Customer Service Driver

- Delivered products in North East area
- Loaded van following order sheet
- Maintained delivery records and logs
- Worked flexible shift system

1993–1995
Various
Provided temporary and emergency cover for general driving and delivery work for agencies.

Education and training:

J&B Training (for NE Central Health Trust)
Passenger Carrying Vehicle Licence

Allerton Secondary School
Four GCSEs, including Maths and English

Personal details:

Date of birth:	6 April 1977
Interests:	Jazz and music in general Fell-walking Railway and transport enthusiast
Health:	Non-smoker
References:	Available on request

Diane Donnelly
Flat 1
121 East Hadbrook Gardens
London NW12 5TT

Tel: 000 000 00000
e-mail: ddonnelly@anyisp.com

Career profile

A competent, reliable dental hygienist experienced in preventative dental care, with excellent interpersonal skills and a clear understanding of the place of oral hygiene in maintaining dental health. A confident, personable individual with experience of working in both private practice and a busy health centre, capable of making a significant contribution to any practice.

Key strengths

Experienced: I have four years' experience as a dental hygienist working in a busy city dental practice and a health centre offering a full range of dental services. I also have four years' experience as a dental nurse working for a prestigious private practice. During this time I have gained my Diploma in Dental Hygiene and Certificate of Proficiency in Dental Nursing.

Able to put patients at their ease: my current job brings me into contact with a wide range of people of all ages and backgrounds and with a variety of dental needs. I use a wide spectrum of communication and interpersonal skills to negotiate their full co-operation and ensure that their experience is as pleasant and effective as possible.

Key skills

- Assessing patient dental health
- Instructing patients on dental health care
- Demonstrating oral hygiene techniques
- Removing tartar, calculus and plaque
- Effecting preventative dental care procedures such as fissure and pit sealing
- Taking and developing dental X-rays
- Administering local anaesthesia
- Providing temporary dressings
- Removing stitches following dental surgery

Key qualifications and experience

- Diploma of Dental Hygiene
- Certificate of Proficiency in Dental Nursing

Diane Donnelly (cont.)

Career summary

The Penn Clinic
2005 to present
Dental Hygienist

Brittain, Rayne & Folks
2003 to 2005
Dental Hygienist

Portway Partners
1998 to 2003
Dental Nurse

Topwell Health Centre
1997 to 1998
Dental Receptionist

Education and training

City Central Dental Hospital

- 2003 – Diploma of Dental Hygiene
- 2000 – Certificate of Proficiency in Dental Nursing

St James Secondary School
GCSEs:
Five including English and Human Biology

Personal details

Date of birth:	17 October 1981
Health:	Non-smoker
Licence:	Full, clean UK driving licence
Interests:	Theatre and cinema
References:	Available on request

Peter Ruckerby
4 Tiverton Lane
Cresslow Common
Buckinghamshire
BK7 2WW

Tel: 0000 0000000

Career profile

A versatile, reliable groundsworker, gardener and maintenance operative with experience of delivering professional maintenance services for first-class contractors. Proficient at planning own schedules and working on own initiative as well as being able to follow instructions accurately. Hardworking and trustworthy, with the proven ability to remain good-humoured and unflappable under pressure.

Key skills

- Institute of Groundsmanship Qualified
- Five years' experience with established maintenance company
- Experience of recreational and sports grounds maintenance
- Full clean UK driving licence
- Able to work 'on call' rota

Career history

2004 to present
Cornwallis Building & Maintenance Contractors
Maintenance Operative
Provided a top-quality maintenance service to a variety of clients in the Buckinghamshire area.
Work undertaken included:

- Basic daily maintenance and preventative repair of properties
- Routine building improvements and repairs
- Carpentry
- Painting and decorating
- Completed service and maintenance logs for each site

Groundsman
Carried out grounds maintenance for two sites
Work undertaken included:

- General seasonal maintenance of grounds
- Maintenance duties:
  - Mowing, rolling and marking
  - Use of pesticides and fertilisers
  - Use of machinery, tools and plant
  - Use of ride-on and gang mower

Peter Ruckerby (cont.)

- Horticultural duties
  - Tree and shrub planting and pruning
  - Turfing
  - Propagating, planting and plant husbandry

2000 to 2004
South Berkshire and District Leisure Department
Groundsworker Manual 3

1996 to 2000
Hayes & Heartcliffe Environmental Services
Groundsworker Manual 1

Education and training

North Buckinghamshire College of Education
Institute of Groundsmanship: National Practical Certificate

1988–1993 Clevedon School
GCSEs:
Five including Maths and English

Personal details

Date of birth:	18 January 1977
Health:	Non-smoker
Interests:	Squash, swimming. Member of the local rugby team
Licence:	Full, clean UK driving licence
References:	Available on request

Paul Colston
71 East Gate, Hadworth
York YK7 4DP

Tel: 0000 0000000
e-mail: pcolston@anyisp.com

Career profile:

A logical and methodical warehouse supervisor with an excellent health and safety record and experience of both warehousing and counter service. An adaptable team worker also willing and able to take responsibility for efficient team productivity.

Key strengths:

Working knowledge of warehouse management: seven years' experience of warehousing; currently manage and support the Inventory Record Accuracy System and the IRA team supplying four sites to ensure stocks of materials are correct and present before production to prevent line down time and support OEE improvements.

Supervisory skills: currently achieve all departmental and site KPIs by implementing policies and procedures that ensure the department functions in an efficient manner in line with agreed KPIs. Monitor the performance of 15 staff to identify training needs and increase productivity. Encourage and promote good team spirit.

Key skills:

Experienced in all aspects of receiving, storing, retrieving and sending out goods:

- Supervising up to 15 staff and checking goods in and out
- Arranging most efficient use of storage locations
- Order picking and assembling:
  - working from order sheets
  - noting inconsistencies
  - checking state of stock
  - reordering as necessary
- Packing and dispatching:
  - assembling orders
  - preparing for transport – postage or delivery
- Store-keeping:
  - selling parts as trade counter assistant
  - maintaining computerised record system
  - using computer terminal and checking printouts to assess availability of parts
- NVQ level 2 – Wholesaling, Warehousing and Stores

Paul Colston (cont.)

Career summary:

2004 to present
Auto City Supplies Ltd
Warehouse Supervisor
Warehouse worker

2000 to 2004
Northern Stores Ltd
Warehouse Worker

1998 to 2000
H Pearson McDuff
Warehouse Worker
Shelf Stacker

1997 to 1998
Various
Shelf Stacker
General Assistant

Education and training:

South Yorkshire College (day release)

- NVQ level 2 – Wholesaling, Warehousing and Stores
- NVQ level 1 – Wholesaling, Warehousing and Stores

Edmund Fairview School

- Six GCSEs, including Maths

Personal details:

Date of birth: 9 June 1981

Licence: Full, clean UK driving licence

Interests: All team sports. Captain of Hadworth and District Cricket Team

References available on request

10

CVs for creative jobs

Creative people provide solutions to problems.

It's the creative person's job to use their technical skill and expertise – whether in design, graphics, engineering or whatever – to achieve tangible results with originality and flair.

Most creative vacancies will require evidence of your creative skills by way of a portfolio of examples. It's important that your CV puts these creative skills in context and emphasises your ability to deliver work of a similar quality, reliably and professionally. The most important area to emphasise, therefore, is your past experience of doing this, which will be a good indication of your ability to do so again in the future.

The key qualities employers usually require in creative personnel are:

- a thorough understanding of your specific field;
- the ability to come up with effective solutions to problems;
- competence, and dependably high standards;
- the ability to work both individually *and* with a team to achieve results;
- flexibility, energy and enthusiasm.

What will get these characteristics across to a prospective employer?

Career profile

An idea of what you have done and how you have done it will be useful in assessing your knowledge and experience.

Key experience

Technical and practical competence and experience are key requirements in creative jobs; it's only when they are present that style and originality can develop. Outline the range of skills you have, and expand on your achievements. This will help an employer to assess your probable future performance.

Career history

Your experience of encountering and solving problems is important. Give details of the skills you have developed in different jobs.

The examples on the following pages show an outline CV including a Key experience section, and CVs that make use of some or all of the above points:

1. **Outline CV.**
2. **Rosa Devon** – Interior and exhibition designer.
3. **Alan Moorhouse** – Writer and broadcaster.
4. **Hannah Gansa** – Editorial assistant and photographer.
5. **Luke Jump** – Graphic artist.
6. **Barbra Kingdom** – Video maker.

The first CV also shows the job ad it was written for.

(**Your Name** in large, bold type)
(Your full address)

____
____
____

(Postcode)

(Telephone number, including area code)

(e-mail address)

Career profile

(A brief, businesslike description of yourself)

(Personal qualities)

(Experience)

(Creative skills and strengths)

Key strengths

(Your skills, experience and personal qualities that most closely match the job requirements)

Key experience

- (Your main areas of experience)
- (Particularly where appropriate to the job you are applying for)
- ______________________
- ______________________
- ______________________

Career history

(**Name of company**, usually starting with the most recent)

(Dates you worked there)

(Job title)

(Brief description of what you did)

(Brief description of what you achieved in this position)

- ______________________
- ______________________
- ______________________

(**Name of company**)

(Dates you worked there)

(Job title)

(Brief description of what you did)

(Brief description of what you achieved in this position)

- ______________________
- ______________________
- ______________________

Name (cont.)

(Name of company)

(Dates you worked there)

(Job title)

(Brief description of what you did. Jobs you did some years ago require less detail than your more recent ones)

Education and training

(Professional training)

(Details of any professional training undertaken at work)

- (Qualification or skill achieved)
-
-
-
-

(Membership of professional bodies)

(or institutes)

(Name of school, college, or university) (Starting with the highest, most recent OR most relevant qualification)

(Dates you attended)

(The qualification you achieved)

(Name of school, college, or university)

(Dates you attended)

(The qualification you achieved)

(Name of school, college, or university)

(Dates you attended)

(The qualification you achieved)

(Don't go back further than your senior or secondary school)

Personal details

(Date of birth)

(Driving licence)

(Married or single – only if relevant)

(Nationality – only if relevant)

(Interests and activities. Brief details)

(References – usually 'available on request')

Interior Designer (mid-weight)

London-based Design Company specialising in furniture, products and interiors is looking to hire an Interior Designer who would be able to work with flexibility on a diverse range of design projects.

The ideal candidate will have a strong knowledge of interior design and project management, including liaising with clients and vendors, producing specification documents, overseeing construction administration, and managing a team (two to three years' experience preferable).

Computer skills will include AutoCAD, Graphite, Adobe Creative Suite, Microsoft Office.

Model-making skills are required, as is the ability to create presentation documents for client presentations.

Reply with CV to Paul Hodge at ____________________

See how Rosa Devon used this job ad to target her CV on the next page.

Rosa Devon
31 Verdon Villas
Spring Gate Heath
Essex EX12 7YC

Tel. 0000 0000000
E-mail: rdevon@anyisp.com

Career profile:

An experienced designer with a background in retail display and domestic design, and a sound understanding of detailed specification, planning and budgeting, and liaising with both clients and subcontractors.

Key skills:

Knowledge of interior design/project management: designed and managed 10 medium to large-scale projects to a high degree of client satisfaction. Adept at liaising with clients, suppliers and local contractors. Previously, six years' experience heading team designing and installing showroom exhibitions for a major furniture retailer.

Flexible: responsible for a wide variety of projects including listed buildings, show homes, a pleasure cruiser and a children's day centre. Flexible and adaptable in order to bring diverse projects in on time and to budget. Experienced at working to a range of budgets and client considerations, and enjoy the challenge of the unexpected.

Computer skills: AutoCAD, Graphite, Adobe Creative Suite, Microsoft Office. I also have experience of 3D model-making.

Key experience:

- Overall management of refurbishment of specialist retail outlet, having responsibility for:
  - Design
  - Planning
  - Budgeting
  - Materials specification
  - Purchasing
  - Hiring subcontractors
- Successfully designing and planning over two dozen shop-floor and point-of-sale exhibitions for a home-furnishing retail chain
- Establishing a successful interior design service in conjunction with a local furnishing store
- Designing, specifying and supervising interior renovation of two Grade II listed properties in heritage area
- Bringing the project in on budget and contributing to a £100k profit for the developer

Career history:

2003 to present: Self-employed
Designer and decorator
Designed domestic and retail interiors:

Rosa Devon (cont.)

- Assessed client requirements
- Negotiated fees and budget with client
- Selected suitable wall coverings, furnishings and fabrics
- Presented proposals to clients
- Bought from UK and overseas sources
- Created specialist decorative paint finishes
- Liaised between client and subcontractors
- Worked to pre-agreed timescale and budget

1998–2003: Marc D'Araby Furniture Galleries Ltd
Display Designer
Designed showroom and point-of-sale displays for retail chain throughout the South of England:

- Assessed requirements of individual store managers
- Designed 'customer-friendly' display settings
- Drew up fully detailed plans and instructions for installation by local contractors
- Supervised final stages and set dressing
- Maintained, renovated and updated displays

1993–1998: Sollways of Liverpool
Display Designer
Window Dresser
Undertook window dressing, in-store display and promotion of home and garden products as part of display team for large city-centre department store.
Promoted to Display Designer in 1996.

Education and training:

1991–1993: City College
Retail Display Certificate Course
Marketing and Retailing
Retail and Retail Display
Point-of-Sale Merchandising
Advertising and Promotion

1986 to 1991: East Faringdean School
Five GCSEs, including Maths and English

Personal details:

Date of birth:	8 June 1975
Interests:	Member of the South of England Watercolour Society and the Women Mean Business Club. Enjoy dancing and antique collecting

Car owner/driver with full, clean UK licence

Alan Moorhouse
23 The Avenue
Seaton Parva
Hampshire HA3 6TL

Tel: 0000 0000000

Career profile:

A writer and broadcaster with a total of 15 years' experience, including 7 years as a regular contributor to Radio Hampshire. An effective communicator with a track record of successful books, articles and radio pieces on local history and regional issues, based on a thorough understanding of journalism.

Key experience:

Writing

- Researching and writing *Buckler's Hard* – the story of Henry Adams, Nelson's ship-builder
- Compiling three local guidebooks:
  - *Romsey Rambles*
  - *Winchester Wanders*
  - *Portsmouth Parade*
- Editing Tourist Board publications:
  - *Days Out on the South Coast – Portsmouth and District*
  - *Days Out on the South Coast – The New Forest*
- Writing a regular 'Local Heroes' column for *Portsmouth Pickings*
- Contributing over 100 articles on local history and natural history for the *South Hampshire Chronicle* and *Points Around* magazine

Broadcasting

- Dramatising *Buckler's Hard* for Radio Hampshire
- Broadcasting regular 10- and 20-minute reports on items of local interest on 'Out and About'
- Writing and presenting 30-minute promotional video for Southcrest Hotels, 'Blow the Man Down'

Career history:

2000 to present
Freelance Writer
Clients include:

- Hampshire Press Ltd
- Tourist Information Board
- Tourist Services Ltd
- Portsmouth Gazette Publications
- Southcrest Holdings Ltd
- Radio Hampshire
- Daniel Deckland & Co Ltd

Alan Moorhouse (cont.)

1997–2000
South Downs Heritage Centre
Publications Manager
Compiled, catalogued and promoted publications of interest to visitors to the Heritage Centre, and for use as a local information resource.

1988 to 1997
South Hampshire Chronicle
Features Editor
Reporter
Edited newspaper articles on local events. Researched and wrote regular column. Reported on local issues. Promoted to Features Editor in 1989.

Education and training:

1986–1988 College of Trade and Commerce
Diploma in Journalism

1982–1985 South Eastern University
BA History and English

1975–1982 Oversands High School
A levels: English History French
GCSEs: eight including English and Maths

Personal details:

Date of birth:	17 August 1964
Interests:	Natural History
	Member of South Down Botanical Society
	Member of the Tallinger local history group
	Voluntary tutor on the local literacy initiative scheme

Car owner/driver with full, clean UK licence

References available on request

Hannah Gansa
Flat 4, Tily Court Mansions
London SW9 0PP

Tel: 0000 000000
e-mail: hgansa@fairport.co.uk

CAREER PROFILE

An experienced assistant editor and photographer with a background in specialist craft books and magazines. Possessing a high degree of technical competence and a commitment to quality, I am now looking for a challenging position where these can be used to maximum effect.

KEY STRENGTHS

Commitment to quality: currently responsible for commissioning the high-quality graphics for which field leader Fairport Magazines is known; instrumental in team that won the Publishing Award two years running.

People skills: have worked profitably with a wide range of people, liaising successfully with editors, suppliers, authors and freelance contributors. Able to question, consult, negotiate and influence to gain understanding of the client's needs using a wide spectrum of approaches to ensure that both editors and contributors feel happy with the outcome.

KEY EXPERIENCE AND ACHIEVEMENTS

- Planning and implementing visual policy for two leading magazines
- Developing key areas within the subject field
- Winning 'Craft Magazine of the Year' two years in succession
- Successfully implementing editorial policy
- Liaising tactfully with authors and freelance contributors
- Designing and co-writing promotional material
- Co-ordinating public relations, publicity and press releases

---

CAREER HISTORY

2005 to present
Fairport Magazines Ltd
Needles and Threads
Happy Hands
Assistant Editor/Photographer
Designed and organised photographs and photographic policy for the magazines:

- Designed, set up and photographed spreads
- Organised and photographed 'step-by-step' instruction series in conjunction with craftspeople
- Edited freelance submissions to journal standard
- Researched and developed new fields of interest to readership
- Solicited contributions from craft-workers
- Covered exhibitions and conventions for news items, ideas and information
- Organised and carried out interviews and photographic sessions with subjects

Hannah Gansa (cont.)

2001 to 2005
Cotswolds Crafts Publications Ltd
Editorial Assistant
Prepared written material for publication:

- Reviewed copy for errors in spelling, syntax and punctuation
- Ensured manuscripts conformed to house style and editorial policy
- Conferred with authors regarding copy changes
- Marked copy for typesetting using standard symbols
- Selected and prepared photographs and illustrations

1998 to 2001
Berholt Freeman Ltd
Marketing Assistant
Assisted with company marketing and promotion:

- Produced annual report, press releases, newsletter, and brochures
- Liaised with ad agencies, printers, art directors, audio-visual and video producers
- Co-ordinated public relations exercises
- Organised inclusion in exhibitions and trade shows

1996 to 1998
Dollar Holdings
Secretary to Marketing Department

- Provided secretarial cover for the department
- Assisted marketing personnel where appropriate

EDUCATION AND TRAINING

Three Acres College of Art and Technology
2003 to 2005 (part-time)
Certificate of Photographic Studies

Sperring Sixth Form College/CFE
1994 to 1996
RSA II Secretarial Certificate
A levels – English, Art, French

Turnall Secondary School
1989 to 1994
GCSEs – six including English and Maths

PERSONAL

Date of birth:	1 May 1978
Health:	Non-smoker
Licence:	Full, clean UK driving licence
Interests:	Member of local amateur orchestra Music appreciation Swimming Aromatherapy
References:	Available on request

Luke Jump

56 Ballard Place, Ashworthy
Oxfordshire OX14 5LA

Tel: 0000 0000000 e-mail: ljump@brand.co.uk

Career profile

Experienced graphic artist with the proven ability to understand client requirements and deliver effective creative solutions within specified deadlines, the ability to use modern technology in the production of graphic material and a wide range of traditional skills, along with well-developed communication skills honed by extensive dealings with senior management and other professionals.

Key skills

Creative drive: successful and award-winning campaigns include 'Beat the Clock' for Em Kay, 'Up and Running' for Game+, 'Pop-pop' for PeopleNet, and 'Ticket to Write' for ESC. Director of Media Standard award agency.

Leadership skills: track record of eight years of motivating an award-winning team to establish and achieve challenging goals and demand the very best from themselves. Feedback from teams demonstrates a confident, vigorous style of leadership based on sincere consultation allied with vision and clear direction.

Communication skills: extensive experience of consultation with client companies; personally conduct client presentations; negotiate with suppliers; consult with team and freelance staff.

Key experience

- Working with Macintosh graphics packages:
  - QuarkXpress
  - Illustrator
  - Photoshop
- Working with four-colour reproduction
- Liaising, consulting and negotiating with clients, including:
  - LLK
  - Employment Services Commission
  - Playnet Computers
  - Kase UK
- Art director of agency winning 'Media Standard' award 2006 and 2008

Career history

2006–present
Brand Response
Art Director
Devised concepts and supervised staff in preparing layout designs for artwork and copy for direct marketing agency:

- Consulted with client companies with regard to aims and objectives, presentation and budget
- Formulated layout and design concept
- Produced, selected or arranged to have produced suitable material for artwork and/or illustrations

Luke Jump (cont.)

- Supervised staff preparing layouts for printing
- Approved final layout for presentation to client

2004–2006
Wells Strata Deanery
Assistant Studio Manager
Assisted organisation and running of studio together with production of high-grade computer graphics for audio-visual company:

- Created a range of graphics for flipcharts, OHP, 35 mm, video presentations and slide animations
- Supervised allocation of projects
- Briefed and monitored freelance staff

News Review Publications Ltd
2002–2004
Designer
Produced graphic material for company bulletins, brochures, annual reports and in-house magazines

PAC Magazines Ltd
2001–2002
Paste-up Artist
Produced paste-ups and mechanicals for magazines

Education and training

Work-related training:
Quark Xpress
Photoshop
Illustrator

South Counties College of Art and Design
1997–2000
Diploma in Art and Design

John Galliard School
1990–1997
A levels – English, Art
GCSEs – six including English and Technical Drawing

Personal details

Date of birth:	16 September 1979
Licence:	Full, clean UK driving licence
Interests:	Marathon running Swimming Hill walking and climbing
References:	Available on request

Barbra Kingdom
41A Pine Court Gardens, Landschurch
Avon AV5 1MR

Tel: 0000 0000000
e-mail: bkingdom@anyisp.com

Career profile:

Innovative and intelligent video maker with experience gained designing and producing videos for a broad range of clients. Adept at working with a wide variety of people effectively and good-humouredly in sometimes demanding situations. Skilled at evaluating and resolving problems creatively.

Key strengths:

Working with people: have worked successfully with a wide range of people, including some quite challenging groups. Able to question, consult, negotiate and influence to gain understanding of the client's needs using a wide spectrum of approaches to ensure that the client feels happy with the outcome.

Technical expertise: comprehensive practical experience based on HND Media and Visual studies training. For full range of expertise – please see below.

Key experience:

- Video and Film
  - Producing and directing seven 30- to 60-minute videos for The Parenting Initiative, including 'Baby Talk', 'Little White Lies' and 'Babyland'
  - Deciding with featured expert the content and presentation of the topic on video
  - Planning lighting, camera angles, camera shots
  - Assisting youth group making youth and community videos
  - Training them in use of equipment and basic production and editing
  - Designing, producing and directing two independent video shorts, 'Moon' and 'All Sorts', shown at the Arts South West Film Festival

- Editing
  - Machine-to-machine video editing
  - Digital and online editing
  - Co-ordinating sound, content and storyline
  - Dubbing
  - Super 8 film viewing, editing and splicing

- Radio
  - Researching, planning and presenting weekly community arts slot on local radio
  - Delivering reports
  - Selecting, approaching and interviewing guests

Barbra Kingdom (cont.)

Career history:

2003 to present
Video Maker
Community Production Facility

Radio Producer and Presenter
Valley Radio

Video Trainer/Facilitator
Kids TV
Community Youth Group

Education and training:

1999–2003 Wessex College of Art and Technology
BTEC HND Media and Visual Studies

Vocational Studies:
The Moving Image
Twentieth Century Film
The National Film Archive

1992–1998 East Faringdean School
GCSEs – five, including English Language
A levels – English and Art

Personal details:

Date of birth: 15 September 1981

Interests: Film, video and music

Car owner/driver with full, clean UK licence

References available on request

11

CVs for clerical and administrative jobs

Clerks and administrators ensure that an organisation runs smoothly and efficiently. It's important that a prospective employer reading your CV believes that you will, first and foremost, take over the vacancy smoothly, effectively and as proficiently as possible, with very little disruption to the department. The most important areas to emphasise, therefore, are your current skills and past experience as these will be the best guide to your future performance.

The key qualities employers usually look for in applicants for clerical and administrative jobs are:

- organisation;
- dependability;
- a methodical approach;
- the ability to work with others;
- specific technical skills;
- experience in specific areas.

What are the main points, then, for a clerical and administrative CV?

Key skills

Many clerical, administrative and secretarial jobs call for specific skills such as word-processing or bookkeeping skills, use of a particular sort of switchboard, use of particular computer software packages, or knowledge of a specific language.

Include all your relevant skills, and highlight the specific skills required for the position in your Key skills section so that they can be clearly seen.

Key experience

Experience in a specific field is often a job requirement – a computer services administrator will have a different area of knowledge and expertise from a personnel administrator. Include experience such as supervision and planning that will be relevant to most positions, then choose key experience – payroll procedures, customer services, whatever – to fit the job you are applying for.

Career history

Concentrate on areas of responsibility, skills used and experience gained. Include improvements in departmental efficiency you have introduced.

Some people find that their clerical or administrative jobs have been essentially similar in content. In this case concentrate on emphasising Key skills and Key experience and simply summarise your actual Career history.

The examples on the following pages show an outline CV that includes both a Key skills and a Key experience section, and CVs that make use of some or all of these points:

1. **Outline CV.**
2. **Amanda Barwell** – Clerical assistant.
3. **Tessa Dixon** – Secretary.
4. **Valerie Andrews** – Secretarial and financial administrator.
5. **Philip McVickery** – Information technology administrator.
6. **Rose Mary Tan** – Records administrator.

(**Your Name** in large, bold type)
(Your full address)

(Postcode)

(Telephone number, including area code)

(E-mail address)

Career profile

(A brief, businesslike description of yourself)
(Personal qualities)
(Experience)
(Skills and personal strengths)

Key strengths

(Your skills, experience and personal qualities that most closely match the job requirements)

Key skills

- (The main skills you have developed)
- (Particularly those appropriate to the job you are applying for)
-
-

Key experience

- (Your main areas of experience)
- (Particularly those appropriate to the job you are applying for)
-
-

Career history

(**Name of company**, usually starting with the most recent)
(Dates you worked there)
(Job title)
(Brief description of what you did)

(Brief description of what you achieved in this position)

-
-
-

(**Name of company**)
(Dates you worked there)
(Job title)
(Brief description of what you did)

(Brief description of what you achieved in this position)

-
-

Name (cont.)

(Name of company)

(Dates you worked there)

(Job title)

(Brief description of what you did. Jobs you did some years ago require less detail than your more recent ones)

Education and training

(Starting with the highest, most recent OR most relevant qualification)

(Name of school, college, or university)

(Dates you attended)

(The qualification you achieved)

(You could include brief details of what was covered in the course, especially if recently qualified)

-
-
-
-
-

(Name of school, college, or university)

(Dates you attended)

(The qualification you achieved)

(Name of school, college, or university)

(Dates you attended)

(The qualification you achieved)

(Don't go back further than your senior or secondary school)

(Professional training)
(Details of any professional training undertaken at work)

- (Qualification or skill achieved)
-
-
-
-

Personal details

(Date of birth)

(Driving licence)

(Married or single – only if relevant)

(Nationality – only if relevant)

(Interests and activities. Brief details)

(References – usually 'available on request')

Are you an experienced Accounts Clerk?
Do you have outstanding clerical and computer skills?
Do you want to work for a small, friendly, successful company?

Our City Centre client is looking for an experienced Accounts Clerk. The role requires previous accounts office experience and will involve preparing accounts, processing and coding invoices, raising and receipting purchase orders, processing invoice payments, period end including prepayments and accruals, preparing profit and loss reports, and dealing with any variances.

The successful candidate will have solid office experience and a professional, confident manner.

This is a great opportunity to work for a successful company in a much-sought-after location.

Reply with your CV to ____________________________.

Amanda Barwell used this job ad to customise her CV so that her suitability for the job would be hard to overlook. She shows how she achieved this on the next page.

Amanda Barwell
5 Juniper Court, Nine Trees
Devon DV22 1JC

Tel: 0000 0000000

Career profile:

Experienced City & Guilds-qualified Accounts Clerk with a comprehensive range of accounts skills and experience of order office and general office administration.

Key strengths:

Outstanding clerical and computer skills: C&G 8953 1 & 2 qualified with five years' experience. Advanced Excel and Access skills; some Sage experience. Comprehensive training in Microsoft Office.

Solid office experience: currently Accounts Clerk for the Languages Department of a large higher education college undertaking a full range of duties and responsibilities, including all those mentioned in the job advertisement. Previously I was an Order Clerk for a busy contracts company responsible for orders and invoicing, and I have several years' experience in other clerical roles.

Professional, confident manner: required to liaise with other departments and members of staff to a very high level, as well as with suppliers and contractors.

Key skills:

- preparing accounts;
- preparing statements showing income and expenditure;
- processing sales invoices, receipts and payments;
- checking that accounts are accurate and dealing with variances;
- helping to prepare final accounts; profit and loss accounts and balance sheets;
- using computerised accounting systems;
- providing administrative support to accountants.

Key experience:

- Accounts clerk
  - documenting accounts
  - preparing correspondence
  - processing invoices, cheques, credit and debit notes, payments and receipts
  - inputting data onto computer files
- Order clerk
  - processing orders
  - raising order codes
  - preparing dockets and dispatching emergency orders
  - filing and retrieving dispatch notes, orders and delivery records
- Clerk-typist
  - typing from manuscript – 40 wpm

Amanda Barwell (cont.)

- completing and dispatching reports
- maintaining files
- organising appointments
- cover for reception and switchboard

Career history:

2003 to present
Kellington Park College
Accounts clerk

2001 to 2003
West End Office Contracts Ltd
Order Clerk

2000 to 2001
Dobson Dean & Co Ltd
Clerk-Typist

1998 to 2000
Hindway Ltd
Clerical Assistant

1996 to 1998
Southcross Hospital
Clerical Assistant

Education:

2000 to 2002
East Devon Open Learning Centre

- Microsoft Office
- Pitman Intermediate Office Practice

2003 to 2005
Whitcombe College
City & Guilds, 8953 1 & 2

1991 to 1996
Marsh Cross School

- Seven GCSEs, including Maths, English and Commerce

Personal details:

Date of birth: 19 January 1980
Interests: Aerobics, swimming and walking
Full, clean UK driving licence
References available on request

Tessa Dixon
61 Chantry Hill
Stoke Dean, Essex EX3 5DM

Tel: 0000 0000000
e-mail: tdixon@anyisp.com

Career profile

A highly trained and experienced personal secretary with excellent shorthand and word-processing skills, who has developed, as secretary to the managing director of a prominent property company, first-rate organisational skills and initiative.

Key strengths

Executive support experience: currently confidential secretary to Managing Director; previously personal secretary to Head of Section; five years' executive-level experience in all.

Excellent secretarial skills: total of 10 years' experience working in professional corporate environments, providing full secretarial support including diary management, dealing with overseas clients and screening calls and e-mails; advanced skills in Word, Excel and PowerPoint; good working knowledge of Lotus Notes.

Key skills

Secretarial skills

- Pitman Private Secretary Diploma
- Keyboard – 70 wpm
- Shorthand – 120 wpm
- Audio typing
- Commercial correspondence

Computer skills

- Word
- Outlook Express
- Excel
- Access
- PowerPoint

Experience

- Ten years' secretarial experience in a wide range of environments
- An understanding of business and the secretary's role therein
- A clear commitment to efficiency
- Knowledge of good office practice and procedures
- An established track record in effective office support

Career summary

2005 to present
Heath McIllany Properties
Confidential Secretary
Provided full secretarial support:

Tessa Dixon (cont.)

- Typed letters, memoranda and reports with due regard to confidentiality
- Compiled monthly reports and statistics
- Organised meetings, took and typed minutes
- Arranged accommodation and travel for staff and overseas visitors
- Co-ordinated diary and appointments for MD
- Communicated with overseas clients

2003 to 2005
Dockland Industrial Company
Personal Secretary
Provided secretarial support to head of section:

- Arranged internal and external meetings
- Took minutes at meetings and typed them up along with summaries and reports for other departments
- Organised all resulting correspondence and enquiries
- Liaised with outside agencies in the production of reports

2001 to 2003
Timberland Insurance
Department Secretary
Provided secretarial support for New Business Team

1998 to 2001
Stanegate Holdings Ltd
Personal Secretary
Shorthand Typist

Education and training

Member of the Institute of Qualified Private Secretaries

2004–2006 City Adult Education College (Part-time/evening course)

- Pitman Private Secretary Diploma
- Pitman Commercial Correspondence
- Pitman Shorthand

1996–1998 Westmordale College of Education

- RSA III Typewriting (Distinction)
- RSA III Shorthand and Typewriting Certificate
- RSA III Audio-typing
- RSA II English Language

1990–1995 Clevedon School
GCSEs:
Five including Maths and English

Personal details

Date of birth:	9 October 1979
Health:	Non-smoker
Licence:	Full, clean UK driving licence
Interests:	Theatre and cinema
References:	Available on request

Valerie Andrews
43 Newton Street,
Northampton N14 5ET

Tel: 0000 0000000

Career profile

A well-organised, reliable secretary with extensive knowledge of good office practice, and a wealth of experience in both large and small companies.

Key strengths

Excellent IT and secretarial skills: four years' secretarial experience providing support for two department heads and the Personnel Director; four years' experience managing the administrative side of a busy sales office. College trained and fully proficient in Microsoft Office, including Word and Excel; currently using Windows XP.

Communication skills: As Office Manager, good communication skills ensured the smooth and efficient running of the office. Excellent presentation, both verbal and written, required as confidential secretary to the Director along with the ability to liaise effective with clients and other members of staff in person, by letter and over the phone.

Initiative and flexibility: currently required to prioritise own workload and that of junior staff, and manage administrative organisation effectively. Sales drives and conferences mean working competently and resourcefully under pressure to tight deadlines to meet urgent requirements. Always happy to 'go the extra mile' when necessary.

Key qualifications

- RSA III Typewriting – current speed 70 wpm
- RSA II Audio-typing – current speed 70 wpm
- RSA II Shorthand – current speed 120 wpm
- City & Guilds CLAIT – Microsoft Office

Key experience

Secretarial

- Confidential Secretary to Personnel Director
- Secretary to Finance Manager
- Secretary to Marketing Department
- Preparing reports and correspondence
- Setting up agendas and minuting all departmental meetings
- Organising client presentations and corporate entertainment

Valerie Andrews (cont.)

Administrative

- Responsible for day-to-day running of 10-person department
- Answerable for all secretarial staff administration
- Co-ordinating department work schedules
- Training and supervising junior staff

Financial administration

- Compiling monthly budget reports
- Preparing quantity audits, projections, and financial statements
- Responsible for raising orders and invoicing for office stationery and consumables
- Supervising accounts payable and accounts receivable

Career summary

2005 to present
Heathfield Enterprises Ltd, Northampton
Personal Secretary

1997 to 2005
Somerhill & Hayes Ltd, Ipswich
Office Manager

Tanstead Personnel Ltd, Preston
1993 to 1997
Temporary Secretarial/Clerical positions

Education and training

1990–1993 North Preston College of Education
RSA Secretarial Certificate
RSA Stage II
RSA Stage III

1983–1990 Clevedon School
GCSEs:
Five including Maths and English
A levels:
English, French and Commerce

Personal details

Date of birth:	21 April 1972
Health:	Non-smoker
Interests:	Badminton, swimming. Member of the local Operatic Society
References:	Available on request

Philip McVickery
66 Cleve Way, St Aldans
Leicestershire LE17 8UK

Tel: 0000 0000000 E-mail: pmcvickery@anyisp.com

Career profile

Experienced administrator with budget, IT and premises-management skills and a background in insurance, commerce and non-profit sectors. Seeking the opportunity to use IT skills in a company where they can contribute to a worthwhile outcome.

Key strengths

Excellent IT skills: gained extensive skills in office applications as systems controller maintaining IT facilities. Currently use Microsoft Office.

Initiative: devised and implemented clear administrative procedures for the Trust's office so that information could be filed and retrieved efficiently; traced and acted upon all outstanding bills and invoices, clarifying the financial position; rationalised entry of information onto database with the result that the Trust's business was more accurately represented.

Key qualifications

- Finance for Administrators
  - Budgeting for contract tenders for government funding
  - Budgeting to precise figures
- Computer skills:
  - JSP structured programme design
  - VAX 780 computer system
  - Excel and SuperCalc spreadsheet applications
  - Access database
  - Microsoft Word word processing

Key skills

- Understanding and using information technology
- Interpreting instructions and carrying out policies accurately
- Dealing with people effectively, tactfully and efficiently
- Analysing problems and providing solutions
- Planning work to meet deadlines

Career history

2005–present
Keyline Youth Trust
Administrator
Ran administrative department on a day-to-day basis, including:

- Budget control and petty cash

Philip McVickery (cont.)

- Premises management
- Designed and implemented administrative procedures in office
- Traced and acted upon all outstanding bills and invoices
- Rationalised entry of information onto database with the result that the Trust's business was more accurately represented

2000–2005
JJ Hey Ltd
System Controller
Ran computer system for six offices, including:
- Routine hardware maintenance
- Data backup
- Provided help-desk facility
- Facilitated effective staff usage of all computer facilities
- Monitored printing and stationery costs and implemented cost-effective measures

Lake & Stewart Insurance Ltd
1995–2001
Claims Supervisor
Assessed claims for redundancy insurance, including:
- Maintained cheque issue deadlines
- Supervised up to seven staff members
- Maintained and administered insurance certificate stocks
- Revised wording of unemployment benefit monthly claim forms resulting in 12% reduction in errors
- Established criteria for conversion of clerical claims to computer operation, resulting in minimal disruption for clients

Department of Employment
1989–1994
Clerical Officer
Processed claims for unemployment benefit

Education and training

1984–1988 Chesterfield College of Education
Certificate of Education
Education Theory, English and Drama

1977–1984 Tembury South School
GCSEs:
Five including Maths and English
A levels:
English and Art

Personal details

Date of birth: 9 February 1966

References: Available on request

Rose Mary Tan
4A Sandle Lane, Churchdean
Dorset DR12 3BL

Tel: 0000 0000000

Career profile

A thorough and methodical records administrator, with extensive experience in the verification, storage and retrieval of records both as documents and on computer databases.

Key strengths

Excellent IT skills: comprehensively trained and experienced in all aspects of database and records systems — collection, storage and retrieval as well as first-stage statistical analysis. Currently using Windows XP office applications.

Supervisory skills: currently supervise 10 staff in records administration including induction and training. Devised and implemented new strategy for handling high volumes of data and trained staff accordingly, leading to a substantial decrease in errors and omissions.

Accuracy and attention to detail: retrieve and administer a large volume of medical data and documents, requiring a high degree of accuracy if comprehensive patient records are to be maintained. All inconsistencies are queried and there has been no substantiated complaint in my department in 18 months.

Key qualifications

- Database and record systems: Access; Excel; MediWatch tailored statistical package
- Computer skills: Word; Outlook Express

Key skills

- Maintaining, developing and administering medical records and data systems
- Supervising staff compiling and inputting record data, and storing documents
- Collecting, storing and retrieving patient data
- Formulating strategies for handling high-volume records
- Implementing effective procedures for storage and retrieval
- Developing 'user-friendly' methods for staff processing
- Undertaking first-stage statistical analysis
- Preparing and supplying information for staff and departments

Rose Mary Tan (cont.)

Career history

Porterhouse Hospital Trust
2003–present
Records Administrator
Experienced in all aspects of receiving, storing, retrieving and supplying data:

- Supervised up to 10 staff
- Maintained and updated records and files
- Checked records in and out
- Noted inconsistencies and queried as necessary
- Processed both documents and computerised records and printouts

Fordice Road Health Centre
1999–2003
Administrative Assistant
Provided clerical and administrative support to Centre Administrator:

- Maintained and updated records
- Input and retrieved data and statistical information
- Co-ordinated communication between staff, clinics and clinic users
- Monitored usage of consumables

Department of Employment
1997–1999
Clerical Officer
Clerical Worker

- Processed claims for unemployment benefit
- Maintained and updated client records

Education and training

Blare Petrie College

- Introduction to Computer Literacy
- Working with Spreadsheets
- Working with Databases:
  - introductory to advanced level
  - working with Windows databases

Torburymouth Senior School
GCSEs:
Five including Maths and English

Personal details

Date of birth:	30 March 1981
Interests:	Opera and classical ballet Gardening
References:	Available on request

12

CVs for sales and marketing jobs

Salespeople ensure that a company sells its products and makes a profit. A prospective employer reading your CV is looking for confirmation that you will be able to sell their goods or services and increase profits for them. The most important thing to emphasise, therefore, is your past success in doing this.

The key qualities employers usually look for in applicants for sales jobs are:

- the ability to sell;
- tenacity and perseverance;
- competence;
- the ability to get on with others;
- energy, commitment and enthusiasm.

What will help you get these points across?

Career profile

An idea of the areas you have covered in the past, the sort of experience you have had to date, and your current position in your career will all be helpful information to a potential employer.

If you have experience outside of sales but relevant to the job you are applying for, include it. Buyers like to feel they are dealing with someone who understands what they're talking about.

Key achievements

Companies want salespeople who can work hard and make money. Let them know what you're capable of doing. If you regularly exceed targets, have a habit of increasing profits or always get the most orders, make sure they know about it.

Career history

This is where you can put actual facts and figures to the claims you have made about your achievements. Outline your performance with past companies and expand on your successes, rather than just stating your responsibilities.

The examples on the following pages show an outline CV including a Key achievements section, and CVs that make use of some or all of the above points. Linda Knauf's CV also shows the job ad it was written for.

1. **Outline CV.**
2. **Linda Knauf** – Telesales.
3. **Paul A Hendry** – Retail store manager.
4. **Paige McLeod** – Salesperson and sales manager.
5. **Francis Scott** – Sales/product manager.
6. **Ruth Sefton** – Media executive.

(**Your Name** in large, bold type)
(Your full address)

____
____
____

(Postcode)

(Telephone number, including area code)
(E-mail address)

Career profile

(A brief, businesslike description of yourself)
(Skills)
(Experience)
(Personal strengths)

Key strengths

(Your skills, experience and personal qualities that most closely match the job requirements)

Key achievements

- (The main things you have achieved)
- (Particularly those appropriate to the job you are applying for)
-
-
-

Career history

(**Name of company**, usually starting with the most recent)
(Dates you worked there)
(Job title)
(Brief description of what you did)

(Brief description of what you achieved in this position)

-
-
-

(**Name of company**)
(Dates you worked there)
(Job title)
(Brief description of what you did)

(Brief description of what you achieved in this position)

-

Name (cont.)

-
-

(Name of company)

(Dates you worked there)

(Job title)

(Brief description of what you did. Jobs you did some years ago require less detail than your more recent ones)

Education and training

(Starting with the highest, most recent OR most relevant qualification)
(Name of school, college, or university)

(Dates you attended)

(The qualification you achieved)

(You could include brief details of what was covered in the course, especially if recently qualified)

-
-
-
-
-

(Name of school, college, or university)

(Dates you attended)

(The qualification you achieved)

(Name of school, college, or university)

(Dates you attended)

(The qualification you achieved)

(Don't go back further than your senior or secondary school)

(Professional training)

(Details of any professional training undertaken at work)

- (Qualification or skill achieved)
-
-
-
-

Personal details

(Date of birth)

(Driving licence)

(Married or single – only if relevant)

(Nationality – only if relevant)

(Interests and activities. Brief details)

(References – usually 'available on request')

Experienced Telesales Executive

Our company is one of the UK's leading providers of premier office equipment and we are currently seeking someone with unusually good telesales skills.

You will be responsible for undertaking a range of duties required to ensure the ongoing development and maintenance of the company, including cold-calling prospective clients ranging from small enterprises to blue-chip organisations, booking appointments, reaching weekly targets set by the Sales Manager, following up appointments and re-appointing where necessary.

You will have relevant experience in an equivalent telesales role, be organised, proactive and systematic, and have excellent interpersonal skills and an articulate and friendly telephone manner.

It goes without saying that you are a dedicated team player with drive and initiative.

If this sounds like you, reply with your CV to ________________.

Linda Knauf answered this ad with the CV on the next page. She used the information it contained to tailor her Career profile and Key strengths to show her suitability for the job.

Linda Knauf
Flat 4, 115 Trebarton Road
Colby, Bucks BK11 7CW

Tel: 0000 0000000

Career profile:

Trained telesales professional with eight years' experience selling premier products and services to business and the public.

Key strengths:

Organised, proactive and systematic: achieved results 15 per cent above target by devising and developing an organised, systematic approach that meant every new customer was contacted and all return customers approached after three months for optimum results.

Excellent interpersonal skills: regularly turned negative responses into positive ones using a comprehensive spectrum of skills; achieved highest rate of return business in the company.

Drive and initiative: have achieved steady promotion with each job through self-funded training and the determination to achieve outstanding results. Have devised several initiatives and innovations subsequently adopted by the rest of the team.

Key achievements:

- Consistently meeting and exceeding targets by 10–15%
- Achieving 110% increase in sales for new territory
- Winning 'top team' award for home improvement sales
- Successfully combining customer care service with new business development programme
- Achieving NVQ 2 in Telephone Selling:
  - Gaining customer attention and interest
  - Projecting company image effectively
  - Winning appointments
  - Handling objections positively and professionally

Career history:

2005 to present; Auto Credit Europe plc; **Telesales/Aftercare service**

- Advised customers how to finance their car purchase
- Negotiated with all types of customers
- Worked effectively with field sales team
- Achieved weekly average sales of £25K worth of cover
- Optimised profit opportunities and sales performance, contributing to an overall centre sales increase of 10%
- Increased sales of financial packages and add-on products by 17%

Linda Knauf (cont.)

2003 to 2005; Redhouse Publications; **Advertisement sales**
- Successfully sold advertising space for two best-selling computer magazines
- Operated in a highly competitive environment
- Achieved 15% increase in sales over and above target

2001 to 2003; Laurell Communications Ltd; **Telesales**
- Effectively sold mobile communications systems to businesses
- Assisted in building up new territory in South Midlands
- Achieved 110% new business growth in first year, 40% ahead of target

2000 to 2001; Wallmix Ltd; **Telesales**
- Cold called to arranged appointments for sales team
- Consistently exceeded target calls by 15%
- Consistently exceeded appointments target by 10%

1998 to 2000; D'Arblay Connaught; **Customer Service Advisor**

1996 to 1998; Terrence Farrow & Partners; **Clerical Assistant**

Education:

Auto Credit Europe Training Centre
- NVQ Telephone Selling level 1
- NVQ Telephone Selling level 2

1995 to 1996; Bistock Secretarial College
- RSA Stage I Keyboard Skills
- RSA Stage I Office Skills

1988 to 1995; South West District School
- Five GCSEs, including Maths, English and French
- Two A levels – French and English

Personal details:

Date of birth: 3 May 1977
Health: Non-smoker
Interests: Team sports – Netball
Women's League American Football
Volleyball

Full, clean UK driving licence
References available on request

Paul A Hendry
6 Yellow Stone Crescent, Headford
Staffordshire ST15 6YY

Tel: 0000 0000000

Career profile:

An experienced store manager with a solid background in high-turnover supermarket environments in a wide variety of locations.

Key strengths:

Experienced retail manager: 12 years' substantial experience gained with three high-turnover chains. Successful delivery of KPI and P&L strategies to achieve targets; full vocational training in all aspects of management from health and safety to EPOS.

Market knowledge: thorough understanding of local market requirements attested to by an increase in turnover of around £30,000 in total; constant review and analysis of local competitor activity and development of appropriate marketing strategy leading to sustained 10–15 per cent annual growth.

Change manager: maintained level of turnover in Bath store despite extensive refurbishment by encouraging high level of commitment and focus in staff and making full use of available resources.

Career achievements:

Starfrost Frozen Foods Ltd; 2003 to present
Various locations – four stores in all

Store Manager

- Increased turnover by around £10k in each of three different stores during time as manager
- Regularly achieved turnover of £25k–£40k, depending on store location
- Achieved a record-breaking Xmas turnover of £126k
- Maintained year-on-year increases of 10–15%
- Maintained level of turnover in Bath store despite extensive refurbishment
- Obtained wines and beers licence for two stores
- Improved stock control and shrinkage
- Supervised staff retraining

Freezer-Foods Ltd; 1996 to 2003
Various locations – 10 stores in all

Store Manager

- Increased turnover of Teddington store from £18k to £25k
- Increased turnover from £27k to £35k in Edgware store
- Increased annual turnover by an average of 15–20%

Paul A Hendry (cont.)

- Ensured each store was promoted to a higher division during time as manager
- Successfully handled two cases of gross misconduct
- Promoted from Assistant Manager in 1998

HMS Hollens; 1995 to 1996
Manager
Bar manager on Royal Navy Base, responsible for the day-to-day running of the bar; organised staff, entertainment and administration.

Shield Market Ltd; 1991 to 1995
Grocery Manager
Organised daily running of the department including hiring staff, ordering stock and achieving set targets. Promoted from Assistant Manager.

Hereford Stores Ltd; 1987 to 1991
Assistant Grocery Manager
Organised daily running of grocery department including administration, staff training and customer service.

Various; 1985 to 1987
Sales assistant and warehouse assistant – various positions.

Work-related training:

Starfrost Frozen Foods Ltd:
- EPOS; FAST; OS2; STOP; SAS

Freezer-Foods Ltd Training Centre:
- Customer Care Awareness Course (Certificate)
- Basic Management Techniques
- Business Systems IBM Computer Course
- Instore Management EPOS Computer Course

ShieldCo Training Centre:
- Merchandising to Increase Sales
- Security Awareness
- Stock and Ordering
- Achieving Monthly Targets
- Health and Safety
- Staff Training, Appraisals and Motivation
- Staff Management Techniques

Personal details:

Date of birth:	21 June 1969
Interests:	Squash – local league player; cycling; skiing; water sports; foreign travel and cookery
Licence:	Full, clean, UK licence

Paige McLeod
Flat 2, 18 Brinsley Square
London SE17 7FS

Tel: 000 0000 0000
e-mail: pmcleod@anyisp.com

Career profile

Highly trained salesperson experienced in business-to-business sales and sales management, with a clear understanding of company structures and the decision-making process. A successful, profit-driven individual capable of making a significant contribution to the profitability of any employer.

Key strengths

Professional attitude: 15 years' sales experience with a clear track record of success leading to steady upward promotion. Member of the Professional Sales and Marketing Society and the Institute of Business, Sales and Marketing; diplomas in both Marketing and Management Studies and a certified diploma in Accounting and Finance.

Successful: a consistent track record of success include increasing sales by 15 per cent annually three years running in a heavily subscribed market; achieving a 120 per cent increase in uptake of technical support services, increasing both direct revenue and repeat orders from satisfied clients; winning Top Salesperson Award 2007; leading the highly successful team that won the top company award four times.

Key achievements

- Mildenhall Business Systems: Took region from fourth place to first place in two years by analysing sales statistics and seeing potential for growth, keeping a tight rein on stock and ordering levels; retraining staff in current sales practice.
- The Business Business: Expanded new territory and took it to second place nationally by setting team targets and ensuring they had the resources to meet them.
- Direction Office Machines: Established and developed virgin territory through extensive marketing campaign.

Career summary

Mildenhall Business Systems
2003 to present
Regional Manager
Responsible for seven retail centres.

- Targeted technical support services and increased uptake by 120%
- Consistently exceeded targets
- Raised profile and increased enquiries by 25%
- Increased sales by 15%
- Improved profits by 12% overall
- Monitored sales statistics and controlled stock levels and ordering
- Assessed and trained sales staff

Paige McLeod (cont.)

The Business Business
1999 to 2003
Sales Manager
Responsible for own territory plus sales team of five people:

- Increased overall profits by 7–15%
- Consistently met and exceeded personal sales targets
- Set team sales budgets, assigned territories and targets
- Undertook staff reviews and training

1994 to 1999
Direction Office Machines
Sales Executive

- Developed virgin territory
- Exceeded target performance by 5%
- Planned marketing campaigns for sales promotion
- Achieved 55% increase in enquiries at peak of promotion

1992 to 1994
Brook Copiers Ltd
Sales Executive

- Exceeded all area sales targets
- Achieved Top Twenty National Sales Award

1988 to 1992
Various
Retail Sales
Telesales

Education and training

Member of the Professional Sales and Marketing Society
Institute of Business, Sales and Marketing

- 2004 – Diploma in Management Studies
- 2000 – Diploma in Marketing

Highbank College
- 1993 – Certified Diploma in Accounting and Finance

Pinder Dobson School
GCSEs:
Five including Maths and English

Personal details

Date of birth:	17 October 1972
Health:	Non-smoker
Licence:	Full, clean UK driving licence
Interests:	Theatre and cinema
References:	Available on request

Francis Scott
12 Nuffield Crescent
Bowerby
Sunderland SN6 7ZP
Tel: 0000 0000000

Career profile:

A sales professional with solid experience in sales, marketing and management, and a history of success in both voluntary organisations and the private sector.

Key strengths:

Sales skills: a full range of skills developed over more than a decade in successful sales and marketing. Consistently achieved above-target sales and trained others in how to do so based on a customer-focused approach that attracted repeat orders from key customers on an ongoing basis.

Presentation skills: currently required to give effective yet enjoyable talks and presentations to the public, the media and other interested bodies to raise awareness of the Wellness Initiative and secure donations. Donations last year totalled £3.5 million.

Leadership: a track record of over 10 years of motivating teams to set and achieve challenging targets and expect the very best from themselves. Feedback from teams demonstrates a confident, vigorous style of leadership based on sincere consultation allied with clear direction.

Key skills:

- Managing accounts and maintaining long-term customer relationships
- Motivating, developing and recruiting staff, including staff training and incentives
- Planning and controlling sales resources to maximum effect
- Maintaining cash flow and profitability
- Analysing and evaluating sales results
- Planning and implementing public relations and advertising campaigns

Career achievements:

2003 to present; The Wellness Initiative
Area Manager
Managed North East region of national medical charity:

- Worked towards Institute of Management NVQ level 4
- Took over and re-established area that had fallen into neglect
- Built up team of trained, professional volunteers
- Established efficient collection service
- Produced and implemented marketing plan
- Improved methods of forwarding donations

2000 to 2003; Dakk & Taylor Ltd
Sales/Product Manager

- Organised and established new product range from concept to completion

Francis Scott (cont.)

- Took over two neglected product ranges and revitalised them
- Organised continuous training programme for internal and external sales personnel with training in sales and product knowledge
- Planned and organised exhibitions and seminars
- Prepared and delivered presentations at all levels, including hands-on product demonstrations to groups of all sizes
- Directly responsible to the Managing Director and Sales and Marketing Director for all aspects relating to the promotion and sale of product range

1995 to 2000; Sensor (UK) Ltd
Product Manager

- Successfully increased sales year-on-year
- Maintained profitability of product range
- Organised consistently innovative public relations and advertising campaign
- Introduced and marketed new product ranges
- Trained and managed sales team
- Supervised customer orders and oversaw stock control

1991 to 1995; Avonside Ltd
Sales Manager

- Increased sales turnover
- Introduced new products and marketing ideas
- Recruited and trained sales team

1986 to 1991; FFG Co
Key Account Manager
Sales Representative

- Proven ability as sales representative and promoted to Key Accounts Manager in 1988

Education:

Institute of Management

- NVQ Sales and Marketing Management level 4

Terrence Keeler Secondary School
1978 to 1985

- A level: Mathematics
- GCSEs: seven including Maths and English

Personal details:

Date of birth:	11 March 1967
Health:	Non-smoker
Interests:	Badminton Riding Computing

Full, clean UK driving licence
References available on request

Ruth Sefton
78 Eastway Road, East Reach
Essex
EX11 9AK

Tel: 0000 0000000
e-mail: rsefton@anyisp.com

Career profile

An innovative and intelligent media executive, with extensive experience of both planning and buying in all media.

Key strengths

Creativity: conceived, planned and implemented innovative media buying to remarkable effect for Callmate's 'Got you, babe' campaign, which increased their inquiry rate by 450 per cent and won an Ad-ept silver award.

Market analysis: in order to this achieve effective campaign, analysed target market and discovered lifestyle trend favouring use of low-cost early-morning cable TV slots, thereby obtaining maximum exposure to the target audience for a minimum budget.

Leadership: a consistent record of 'setting the pace' on projects and achieving goals through a balance of consultation and negotiation allied with vision and clear direction, an approach that I am told was instrumental in my achieving promotion within my current agency.

Career history

2004–present
The Advertising People
Media Executive
Assistant Media Planner
Recommended appropriate and effective media for agency clients:

- Participated in preliminary talks with clients alongside Account Executive
- Analysed target market and marketing objectives
- Formulated media strategy
- Prepared detailed media plans
- Negotiated media rates
- Responsible for £2.5 million multimedia television account, and £1.75 million print media account
- Supervised current assistant planner
- Promoted from Assistant Media Planner to Media Executive in 2006

Ruth Sefton (cont.)

2001–2004
Range, Klein and Morrisey
Media Buyer

- Analysed data from NRS and BARB
- Prepared media strategy for direct-marketing clients
- Negotiated with media representatives for best rates
- Kept detailed records of all transactions

1998–2001
The Word Factory
Personal Assistant

- Provided administrative support to Media Director and Media Department

Education and training

North Western University
BA English Literature (2.2)

Edward Marshall School
GCSEs: seven including Maths and English
A levels: English, French and History

Personal details

Date of birth:	21 June 1978
Interests:	Modern dance Fine art and antiques Travel
Licence:	Full, clean UK driving licence
References:	Available on request

13

CVs for technical jobs

Technical personnel are required to carry out processes or production methods smoothly, accurately and efficiently.

It's important that a prospective employer reading your CV believes that you have the technical expertise – the knowledge and experience – to take over the vacancy efficiently, with as little disruption to the department as possible. The most important areas to emphasise, therefore, are your technical competence, experience, and qualifications and training, as these will be the best guide to your likely performance.

The key qualities employers usually look for in applicants for technical jobs are:

- specific technical skills;
- experience in specific areas;
- dependability and accuracy;
- a methodical approach;
- organisation;
- the ability to work with others.

What are the key points that differentiate a technical CV from those for other jobs?

Career profile

Use your Career profile to highlight the experience that brings competence and expertise, which are of value in many technical jobs.

Key qualifications

For many technical positions, your qualifications and training are the most important things you have to offer. However, if you simply move your Education and training section to the front page, you risk being mistaken for a college-leaver without a Career history. The solution is to summarise your education and training in a Key qualifications section on the first page.

Qualifications and training relevant to the job you are applying for take priority. For example, you may be able to use several computer languages, but only the one or two used in *this* job need to go in the summary. The rest can be included in the Education and training section.

Key skills

As well as your Key qualifications, it's a good idea to include a non-academic Key skills section outlining your practical and/or managerial skills and experience.

Career history

Concentrate on the areas of responsibility you have covered, the skills you've used and the experience gained.

The examples on the following pages show an outline CV that includes both a Key skills and a Key qualifications section, and CVs that make use of some or all of these points:

1. **Outline CV.**
2. **James Barossa** – System controller.
3. **Larraine Watt** – Psychology research assistant.
4. **Alison McInnery** – Computer professional.
5. **Robert Murray** – Research Fellow.
6. **John Crabb** – Food technician.

(**Your Name** in large, bold type)
(Your full address)

(Postcode)

(Telephone number, including area code)
(E-mail address)

Career profile

(A brief, businesslike description of yourself)
(Skills)
(Background and experience)
(Career aims)

Key strengths

(Your skills, experience and personal qualities that most closely match the job requirements)

Key skills

- (The main skills you have developed)
- (Particularly those appropriate to the job you are applying for)
-
-

Key qualifications

- (The main qualifications you have)
- (Particularly those appropriate to the job you are applying for)
- (Include membership of professional bodies where relevant)
-

Career history

(**Name of company**, usually starting with the most recent)
(Dates you worked there)
(Job title)
(Brief description of what you did)

(Brief description of what you achieved in this position)

-
-

(**Name of company**)
(Dates you worked there)
(Job title)
(Brief description of what you did)

Name (cont.)

(Brief description of what you achieved in this position)

-
-

(Name of company)

(Dates you worked there)

(Job title)

(Brief description of what you did. Jobs you did some years ago require less detail than your more recent ones)

Education and training

(Starting with the highest, most recent OR most relevant qualification)

(Name of school, college, or university)

(Dates you attended)

(The qualification you achieved)

(Include brief details of what was covered in the course)

-
-
-
-

(Name of school, college, or university)

(Dates you attended)

(The qualification you achieved)

(Name of school, college, or university)

(Dates you attended)

(The qualification you achieved)

(Don't go back further than your senior or secondary school)

(Professional training)

(Details of training undertaken relevant to the work you do)

- (Qualification or skill achieved)
-
-
-

Personal details

(Date of birth)

(Driving licence)

(Married or single – only if relevant)

(Nationality – only if relevant)

(Interests and activities. Brief details)

(References – usually 'available on request')

Data Services Manager

We are an international Customer Services Company and we seek a Data Services Manager to join our team to manage and deliver services to support the efficient and effective operation of the whole business.

You will need to have proven general administration skills and an excellent working knowledge of IT – especially Microsoft Office (including Access and Outlook) and systems management. The successful candidate will ideally be resourceful and ambitious, have good interpersonal skills and be a good communicator, be committed to the highest standards of quality, and be happy working both as part of a team and on their own initiative.

This role will possibly be ideal for a strong Administrator with an interest and key skills within IT. We will consider applicants from IT Support/ Technical backgrounds who are also able to demonstrate the key administrative skills required.

Apply to ________________________________.

Turn to the next page to see how James Barossa used this job ad to give his CV added relevance by incorporating key information from it in his Career profile and Key strength sections.

James Barossa
85 St Luke's Place, Collington
Berkshire BK6 2JZ

Tel: 0000 0000000
e-mail: jbarossa@anyisp.com

Career profile

Versatile and proficient Data Services professional with an administration background and extensive IT support skills. Capable of making a significant contribution to the efficiency of any organisation.

Key strengths

Proven administrative skills and an excellent working knowledge of IT: six years' experience providing full IT support to the South-East division (six offices: 200 staff) of a big insurance company, responsible for all administration associated with that role.

Resourceful, ambitious and committed: improved the efficiency of the system to the extent that claims once taking two weeks to process now take two days. Downtime for faults and malfunctions has decreased from 24 days a year to 3. Undertook HND in own time and expense to further my career and promoted to current position as a result.

Good interpersonal skills/good communicator: liaise between IT staff and the rest of the company at all levels; mentor and train new IT support staff and provide full information about the system status. I use a full range of interpersonal skills to achieve these tasks and also to evaluate user needs and assess problems in user-friendly, non-technical terms.

Key skills

- Ensuring the smooth running of all IT systems, including anti-virus software, print services and e-mail provision, providing users with appropriate support and advice and managing crises
- Supporting, facilitating and encouraging both effective usage and good practice
- Working in close co-operation with users and IT staff to clarify areas for change and development
- Evaluating user needs and system functionality and ensuring that IT facilities meet the needs of individuals and projects
- Planning, developing and implementing the IT budget, obtaining competitive prices from suppliers, where appropriate, to ensure cost-effectiveness
- Researching and installing new systems and scheduling upgrades
- Ensuring data security.

Key qualifications

- City & Guilds Diploma in Computer Applications
  PC Operating Systems – DOS and Windows; Unix; Word; Excel; Access; Outlook

James Barossa (cont.)

Career summary

Perry & Wybrowe Insurance Ltd
2001 to present
System Controller
Supported 200 staff on six sites throughout the South of England using computerised systems:

- Provided help desk for software and hardware queries
- Used VMS and RSX Operating Systems to recover lost data files
- Analysed system performance, identified problems and established probable origin before taking appropriate action
- Logged errors for both software and hardware, and referred on to either programmers or engineer as appropriate
- Installed and implemented communications equipment using X21, Kilostream and Mercury links
- Backed up data records and transferred to off-site storage
- Maintained hardware and data wiring
- Promoted from Claims Supervisor to System Controller after completing City & Guilds training in 2001, in time to oversee computerisation of organisation

Ambassadors Assurance
1996 to 2001
Assistant Claims Supervisor
Clerk

Education and training

Central Berkshire CAT

- 2001 – City & Guilds Diploma in Computer Applications

The Willis School
GCSEs: five including Maths and English

Personal details

Date of birth:	2 January 1980
Health:	Non-smoker
Licence:	Full, clean UK driving licence
Interests:	Collecting early silent films and cine films Member of the English Film Archive
References:	Available on request

Larraine Watt
Flat 3, 14 Deans Gate Road, Waterly
Hertfordshire HE14 3GN

Tel. 0000 0000000
e-mail: lwatt@ncl.ac.uk

Career profile

Psychology graduate with a specific interest in education and development, especially as applied to adult learning, and practical experience of eliciting, collecting and analysing psychological data.

Key strengths

Project design: have co-ordinated, planned and run all stages of experiments including initial design, collecting data using a range of techniques such as observation, interviews and questionnaires; analysing data; writing detailed, comprehensive research reports and presenting the results.

Communication skills: achieving the best data requires tactful and effective communication with subjects, which I always strive for. Presentation of initial ideas requires clarity and confidence if they are to be adopted, while completed reports must present results clearly and intelligibly if they are to be of value.

Initiative and commitment: responsible for initiating and proposing research into effects of stress on learning and carrying through design and implementation of project. Required to prioritise workload and manage day-to-day administrative organisation efficiently, while research projects mean working both competently and resourcefully under pressure to meet defined requirements. I believe colleagues and co-workers would agree that I am always happy to 'go the extra mile' when necessary.

Key qualifications

- MSc The Psychology of Learning
- BSc Psychology
  - Advanced statistical analysis
  - Quantitative techniques in applied research
  - Experimental psychology
  - The psychology of education and development

Career history

North London College
2006–present
Centre for Educational Research
Research Assistant

Conducted research into effects of relaxation and/or stress in learning situations with adult learners:

Larraine Watt (cont.)

- Planned and arranged experiments with aim of providing specific research data
- Took subjects through experimental procedures
- Collected and collated results
- Analysed preliminary data by computer
- Prepared preliminary report on findings

University of East England
2001–2006
Research Assistant
Completed BSc and continued to MSc as research assistant to Professor Henry Jenkins, investigating the role of colour in children's play and development.
Assisted as demonstrator for undergraduate zoology practicals.

Education and training

University of East England
MSc The Psychology of Learning
BSc Psychology (2.1)

Kings Mordent School
GCSEs: eight including Maths, English and Biology
A levels: Biology, Chemistry and Sociology

Personal details

Date of birth:	14 May 1983
Interests:	Singing with local musical society Modern and classical music Yoga
Health:	Non-smoker
Licence:	Full, clean UK driving licence
References:	Available on request

Alison McInnery
91 Southways Road
East Studley
Surrey SR14 4OC
Tel: 0000 0000000
e-mail: amci@anyisp.com

Career profile

An experienced computer professional with a background in software development for structural engineering research and systems management, now specifically interested in the area of water resources or environmental science, and keen to gain experience leading to membership of the Chartered Institute of Water and Environmental Management.

Key skills and qualifications

- MSc Water Environment
- BSc (Hons) Ocean Science
- Mapping environmental, specifically hydrological, information via ARC/INFO Geographical Information System
- Using ORACLE/SQL*Plus database technology
- Pro*Fortran programming and environmental modelling

Career history

NAAC
Institute of Hydrology, Pardham 2006–present
MSc Placement
Mapped river flow data for 1985 drought in Western Europe for completion of MSc dissertation:

- Contributed to UNESCO regional hydrology research project
- Identified gaps in time-series data, providing a basis for future research
- Produced map sequences for Western Europe, aiding presentation of the progress of the drought

Northern Power and Electric
Halford Technology Centre, Nordham, 1999–2004
Second Engineer
Analyst programmer:

- Developed 3-D computer graphics for finite element structural analysis resulting in external sales in the UK and overseas as well as internal use
- Provided CAD system management and technical support for internal and external clients

East Midlands Power Generating Board
Research Division, Stourling, 1993–1999
Technical Officer
Analyst programmer:

- Developed 3-D CAD graphics on IBM mainframe system

Alison McInnery (cont.)

- Analysed data from computerised test rig
- Gave technical support on graphics hardware for engineering research throughout UK on network
- Promoted from laboratory technician in 1996

General employment
1988–1993
- Computer operator
- Mechanical Engineer
- ONC mechanical engineering apprentice

Education and training

2006–present Downland University
MSc Water Environment
- Environmental Information Systems
- Water industry public relations and marketing
- Environmental law
- Project planning
- Operations and finance
- Ecological and adaptive management

2003–2006 University of the South West
BSc (Hons) Ocean Science
- Environmental modelling
- Sedimentation
- Underwater science
- Marine law and resources
- Physical oceanography

1998–2003 Open University
BA Science and Technology
- Computer-aided design
- Geology
- Imaging systems
- Information technology
- Oceanography

Computer skills:
- DEC/VAX and SuperProject system management
- ARC/INFO geographical information system
- Silicon Graphics GL, GraPHIGS and IBM GDDM computer graphics
- UNIX operating system
- FORTRAN and 'C' programming
- Word, Access and Excel

Personal details

Date of birth:	5 June 1971
Licence:	Full, clean UK driving licence
Interests:	Cross-country running, gliding, swimming, sailing
References:	Available on request

Robert Murray
12 Henshaw Place, Upper Tithing
Northamptonshire NP12 3GV

Tel: 0000 0000000
e-mail: rmurray@anyisp.com

Personal profile

A realistic, reliable and open-minded researcher with mathematical, statistical and organisational skills and broad experience in social research. A good team worker with a healthy sense of humour who works well under pressure.

Key strengths

Supervisory skills: supervised junior staff during course of research project, training them in the required techniques and monitoring performance, and have also managed staff in a retail environment.

Communication skills: working with interviewees on such a sensitive subject required patience, tact and diplomacy. Clear and logical report-writing skills and good presentation skills required to present research findings effectively to both a medical and a non-medical audience.

Key skills

- Delivering all stages of a research project
  - Writing proposals
  - Questionnaire design
  - Interviewing
  - Data analysis
  - Report writing and presentation
- Supervising junior staff
- Working with interviewees requiring patience and diplomacy
- Computer-literate – Statistical Package for Social Sciences

Key qualifications

- BA (Hons) Applied Social Studies
- Diploma of the Market Research Society
- Use of Statistics in Medical Sociology
- Quantitative Techniques in Social Research

Career history

2003–present
Northern and Western Medical School
Centre for Research on Drugs and Health Behaviour
Research Fellow
Research Assistant
Conducted research into high-risk (HIV) behaviour of illicit drug users:

- Prepared and designed research project
- Supervised staff

Robert Murray (cont.)

- Interviewed high-risk groups
- Analysed resulting data
- Presented results

The results of this research project and subsequent publication and presentation at conference:

- Validated the use of needle exchange schemes
- Helped attract further funding via other research programmes
- Promoted extension of the scheme with a subsequent increase in staff levels

Rollandson Bookmakers
Tribune Bookmakers
1998–2002 Part-time
1993–1998 Full-time
Manager
Responsible for all aspects of running a betting shop:

- Cash control
- Security
- Managing staff
- Accounts reconciliation
- Dealing appropriately with customers and clients

Education and training

1998–2002 Polytechnic of the City (now City University)
BA (Hons) Applied Social Studies 2:1

- Sociology
- Research methodology
- Computing
- Social policy
- Statistics

1986–1993 Oxhill Grammar School and College of Further Education
GCSEs: seven including Maths and English
A levels: English, French, History

Work-related training:
- Use of Statistics in Medical Sociology:
  applying statistical tests to quantitative data
- Quantitative Techniques in Social Research:
  the application of quantitative techniques

Personal details

Date of birth:	7 November 1975
Licence:	Full, clean UK driving licence
Interests:	Most sports, including football, tennis, golf and snooker
References:	Available on request

John Crabb
1 Ascot Lane, Hills Barton
Cheshire CX14 8JN

Tel: 0000 0000000

Career profile

A food technician and supervisor with experience gained in all departments of food manufacturing from Quality Control to New Product Development, together with a sound understanding of Total Quality Management.

Key strengths

Experience of automated procedures: I currently work for a large, automated producer in a supervisory role, responsible for the continued smooth running of the process and am consequently knowledgeable about all stages of production.

Appropriately qualified: HND in Food Technology from Southlands University; 12 years' experience in food production.

Supervisory skills: currently working as Department Supervisor with overall responsibility for all stages of manufacture and management of eight staff. Reduced downtime in the past year by 7 per cent through staff training and maintenance initiatives.

Key skills and qualifications

- BTEC HND Food Technology
- Extensive knowledge of the food manufacturing industry
- Managing and supervising staff
- Planning and executing product trials to budget
- Implementing laboratory requirements and techniques
- Understanding the importance of marketability and profitability

Professional experience

2001 to present
Cantrip Farms (Production) Ltd
Barton Magna
Department Supervisor

Worked in supervisory role in all areas of yogurt manufacturing from raw material to production through to cold store distribution

- Improved process within natural set department
- Reduced wastage in custard-style yogurt department
- Improved efficiency overall, reducing costs and improving profit margins

John Crabb (cont.)

1999 to 2001
Hilldean Dairies Ltd
Pollend
New Product Development Technician

Developed marketing ideas into manufacturable products

- Developed key product ranges, improving market placement
- Increased product diversity and, consequently, viability within group
- Consistently brought processing trials in to time and on budget

1995 to 1999
Farm Fresh Foods Ltd
Millingham
Senior Laboratory Assistant

Responsible for quality control of all incoming raw materials and supervision of staff in the absence of the Quality Control Supervisor

Promoted from Laboratory Assistant in 1997

Education and training

1989 to 1994

Southlands University
Sunderford
BTEC HND Food Technology

1986 to 1988
Pentland College of Agriculture and Horticulture
Pentland
BTEC OND Food Technology

1981 to 1986
Bower Park School
Alston
Total of five GCSEs gained, including Maths and English

Personal

Date of birth: 10 May 1970
Driving licence: Full, clean UK licence
Health: Non-smoker

Interests

I have a keen interest in sport and keeping fit, and play regularly for a local Sunday football team.

References Available on request

14

CVs for management jobs

Managers ensure that things happen as and when they should within an organisation. It's a manager's job to see that his or her personnel can carry out their own jobs effectively and efficiently.

It's essential a prospective employer believes that you will be an effective manager. It's important, therefore, to emphasise your past achievements in your CV, as these will be a good indication of your future abilities.

The key qualities employers usually look for in applicants for management jobs are:

- the ability to get results;
- the ability to motivate and manage others;
- competence, reliability and responsibility;
- tenacity and perseverance, along with energy, commitment and enthusiasm;
- the ability to tackle problems effectively.

What will help get these qualities across?

Career profile

Personal qualities often count in management positions. Include these in a Career profile to highlight your special characteristics. Outline your own personal style of management and the experience you've had to develop and exercise these qualities.

Key achievements

Companies want managers who can make a difference to performance – achievements matter. Include a Key achievements section, either with or instead of a Key skills section. Let them know what you're capable of doing.

Career history

Put facts and figures to the claims you have made. Rather than just stating your responsibilities, give details of your performance with past companies and expand on your achievements and results.

Your experience of encountering and solving problems is important as well.

The examples on the following pages show an outline CV including a Key achievements section, and CVs which make use of some or all of the above points. Aldwin Hills' CV also shows the job ad it was written for.

1. **Outline CV.**
2. **Aldwin Hills** – Financial manager.
3. **Linda Vernon** – Catering manager.
4. **Mark Renato** – Operations manager.
5. **Ellen Ashe** – Personnel manager.
6. **Lee Daniels** – Technical manager.

(**Your Name** in large, bold type)
(Your full address)

(Postcode)

(Telephone number, including area code)

(E-mail address)

Personal profile

(A brief, businesslike description of yourself)
(Personal qualities)
(Experience)
(Management skills and strengths)

Key strengths

(Your skills, experience and personal qualities that most closely match the job requirements)

Key achievements

- (The main things you have achieved)
- (Particularly those appropriate to the job you are applying for)
-
-

Career history

(**Name of company**, usually starting with the most recent)
(Dates you worked there)
(Job title)
(Brief description of what you did)

(Brief description of what you achieved in this position)

-
-
-

(**Name of company**)
(Dates you worked there)
(Job title)
(Brief description of what you did)

(Brief description of what you achieved in this position)

-
-
-

Name (cont.)

(Name of company)

(Dates you worked there)

(Job title)

(Brief description of what you did. Jobs you did some years ago require less detail than your more recent ones)

Education and training

(Professional training)

(Details of any professional training undertaken at work)

- (Qualification or skill achieved)
-
-
-
-

(Membership of professional bodies)

(or institutes)

(Name of school, college, or university) (Starting with the highest, most recent OR most relevant qualification)

(Dates you attended)

(The qualification you achieved)

(Name of school, college, or university)

(Dates you attended)

(The qualification you achieved)

(Name of school, college, or university)

(Dates you attended)

(The qualification you achieved)

(Don't go back further than your senior or secondary school)

Personal details

(Date of birth)

(Driving licence)

(Married or single – only if relevant)

(Nationality – only if relevant)

(Interests and activities. Brief details)

(References – usually 'available on request')

Business Development Consultant

Are you someone special?
This is a fantastic opportunity to join one of the leaders in providing management solutions. We are known for bringing a variety of skills and experience to meet challenging client requirements and we need a Business Development Consultant to join our team.

You will be pragmatic with a wealth of experience at senior executive level and a bias towards practical solutions with the ability to relate to the needs of a range of businesses.

You may have run your own successful business, held a training role in a corporate or finance business, or have a proven track record in profit responsibility for a medium/large organisation.

You will have excellent communication and interpersonal skills and an outstanding degree of business acumen.

If this sounds like you, send your CV to _______________________.

The next page shows how Aldwin Hills made use of the information in this ad to customise his CV so that it clearly demonstrated his suitability for the job.

Aldwin Hills
7 White Hart Villas, Wood Heath
Norfolk NF11 6DM

Tel: 0000 0000000

Career profile:

LAUTRO-trained financial consultant with a wealth of experience dealing with corporate solutions, a proven talent for business planning and forecasting, and a management background gained in both manufacturing and services.

Key strengths:

A wealth of experience at senior executive level: Eight years' experience at senior management level, including marketing, finance and project management with large and medium-sized organisations.

Outstanding degree of business acumen: Currently running own successful management consultancy advising on budgeting, planning and forecasting in order to improve accuracy, timeliness and efficiency with up to 25 per cent performance increases.

Ability to relate to the needs of a range of businesses: Have provided financial advice, marketing management and project management for a range of organisations from a venture capital company to haulage companies and wholesalers.

Key achievements:

- Improving performance of client organisations by 5–25% overall, including:
  - ABC UK Ltd
  - Xpress Haulage
  - Cornwallis Systems Ltd
- Establishing a venture capital company in the UK on behalf of the parent company
- Bringing the project in on budget and generating £4 million of business in the first three months

Career history:

2003–ongoing
Management Consultant

- Analysed and advised on aspects of business finance:
  - Analysing financial data and monitoring financial control
  - Producing budgets, cash-flow forecasts, and profit and loss projections
  - Analysing and processing productivity records
  - Assisting businesses to develop in a realistic and viable way
- Advised companies wanting to raise finance
- Compiled guidelines and yardsticks for companies wishing to monitor their performance and develop further, including:
  Market segmentation; Financial controls; Production; Product/service development
- Prepared and presented business plans, including break-even analysis

Aldwin Hills (cont.)

Maynard Investment Corporation (Portland International)
2001–2003
Project Manager
Established UK subsidiary for overseas investment corporation:

- Researched and analysed market
- Created venture capital company and established company's presence in the UK
- Installed and implemented all administrative systems
- Administered all documentation, agreements and financial analyses
- Achieved early break-even by keeping well within budget
- Generated over £4 million of business within three months of UK launch

Preston and Fielding
1999–2001
Financial Adviser
Analysed clients' current situations and future goals. Advised and assisted them to plan and monitor their financial situation. Trained and qualified by LAUTRO.

Hoopers Ltd
1995–1999
Sales and Marketing Executive
Sold, marketed and promoted garden products to single and multiple garden centres and similar outlets.

Willings & Cathar Wholesale Blinds Ltd
1980–1995
Sales Director
Started as general assistant and reached director level with responsibility for group.

Work-related training:

Computer skills:
CLAIT
List Manager – Xerox Corporation course on building and maintaining databases
Microsoft Office:
Word; Excel; Access; PowerPoint

Other:
Business Planning and Good Business Practice
Taxation, Annual Accounts and the HMRC
Advertising and Promotion
Marketing – Planning and Implementation
Direct Marketing
Negotiating Skills
Customer Care

Personal details:

Date of birth: 16 September 1964
Interests: Member of the Wood Heath Photographic Society and the Enterprise Business Club, active in the PDSA and the North Norfolk Performing Arts Committee. Enjoy swimming and walking
Car owner/driver with full, clean UK licence
References available on request

Linda Vernon
33 Shortmead Road, Allerton
Derbyshire DB3 5TF

Tel: 0000 0000000

Personal profile

Confident and creative manager with significant experience in both catering and management gained with major employers in the field, and proven skills in setting and achieving goals through the development and motivation of staff.

Key strengths

Restaurant management experience: two years as assistant manager of La Noisette Restaurant with full responsibility for daily functions.

Drive and motivation: promoted steadily from Catering Assistant to Assistant Manager of a leading restaurant, I have never held a job without improving efficiency or bringing in new business. Personally undertook extensive staff retraining programme at La Noisette to make service something truly memorable.

Key skills and achievements

- Six years' experience in restaurant and catering management
- Improving efficiency of service in two significantly different environments
- Successfully introducing comprehensive staff training programmes
- Establishing systems and procedures for a large-scale catering operation
- Managing a first-class restaurant

Career history

2006 to present; **La Noisette Restaurant; Assistant Manager**
Responsible for day-to-day running of restaurant and management of 10 restaurant-area and bar staff.
Duties included:

- budgeting
- stock control
- ordering
- bookings
- customer service

Introduced comprehensive staff training schedules, resulting in a greatly improved service to customers and the continued enhancement of La Noisette's first-class reputation.

2003 to 2006; **Lambourne Health Trust; Catering Supply Manager**
Full responsibility for planning and delivery of catering service to two hospitals, four nursing homes and four residential facilities.

Linda Vernon (cont.)

Duties included:

- full budget planning
- service administration
- management of up to 20 staff

Improvement of service efficiency resulted in reduction of service costs by 12%.

2001 to 2003; **Hollander Catering; Assistant Manager**
Responsible for day-to-day organisation of a commercial catering company including both office and staff administration.
Planned and delivered presentations for company which won two major new contracts.

1999 to 2001; **Cornfleet Country Club; Food Store and Cellar Manager/Banqueting Assistant**
Responsible for supervision of all stock ordering and deliveries for cellars and food stores, and organisation of table layouts for all function rooms.

1997 to 1999; **Various; Waitress/Catering Assistant**
General waitress duties including providing breakfast, lunch and dinner to 550 people daily, and silver service in a five-star country hotel.

Education and training

Professional training
Restaurant and Catering Training Association
NVQ level 3 Catering
NVQ level 3 Catering Management
NVQ level 4 Business Management

Dorning College of Technology
Combe, Dorset; 1995 to 1997
City & Guilds Catering Certificate

Bordingham Comprehensive
Bordingham, Dorset; 1990 to 1995
Total of seven GCSEs, including Maths and English

Personal details

Date of birth:	12 April 1979
Licence:	Full, clean UK driving licence
	Hygiene Certificates held
	St John's Ambulance First Aid certificate held
Interests:	Active member of local environmental group
	Member of the Wine Society
References:	Available on request

Mark Renato
43 Redding Pit Road, Heath Place
West Sussex SX15 8DD

Tel: 0000 0000000
e-mail: mrenato@bishopgroup.co.uk

Career profile:

An Operations Manager with a total of 15 years' manufacturing experience including seven years at senior management level. An effective communicator and motivator with a track record of achievement in implementing change successfully and efficiently, based on a thorough understanding of engineering processes.

Key strengths:

Solution-focused: devised and implemented development plan for two subsidiary factories, increasing efficiency by 12 per cent, which put them on an equal footing with the rest of the company.

Understanding of employee relations and excellent communication skills: required to negotiate effectively with clients and suppliers, including the MOD and Crown Suppliers, as well as other members of staff. Improved long-standing difficulties in industrial relations at acquired site and restored management leadership with a package of measures including a negotiated Partnership Agreement, which increased productivity by 15 per cent.

Self-motivated: committed to a programme of continued vocational training including negotiating skills, office-appropriate IT skills, and management skills.

Key achievements:

- Increasing financial performance of group by £250k overall
- Reducing duplicated operating costs by £100k per annum
- Managing and co-ordinating activities at three factory sites and ensuring efficient supply of products to customers
- Reorganising and establishing Administrative Support Centre
- Drawing up and implementing change programme in two subsidiary factories, bringing them level with rest of group
- Improving industrial relations, restoring management leadership with help of Partnership Agreement

Career history:

2005 to present
Bishop & Challenger Ltd
Operations Manager
Responsible for factories and staff within the operational area.

- Co-ordinated and managed activities within three factories and an Administrative Centre
- Organised efficient running of sites
- Ensured delivery of products to internal and external customers
- Managed quality control, budget and timetable requirements
- Prepared budgets and allocated capital expenditure

Mark Renato (cont.)

2002 to 2005
Deans Valley Forgeway Ltd
Factory Manager
Responsible for all aspects of factory management.

- Achieved budget production levels
- Administered Health and Safety legislation
- Prepared budgets
- Allocated capital expenditure
- Liaised with customers, notably MOD and Crown Suppliers

Esbarten Engineering Ltd
1998 to 2002
Industrial Engineer
Responsible for engineering services at factory and regional level. Provided production engineering service with particular emphasis on product costing, pre-production engineering and methods assessment and improvement.

1994 to 1998
Peckham & Been Associates Ltd
Design and Development Engineer
Designed and developed prototypes from inception through to production. Promoted from apprentice level in 1991.

Work-related training:

Computer skills:
CLAIT
Computer Smartware II
Microsoft Office:
 Word
 Excel
 Access

Other:
Open University – The Effective Manager
City & Guilds – Certificate in Mechanical Engineering
Supplementary Certificates in:
- Toolroom Practices
- Inspection and Quality Assurance
- Health and Safety Legislation
- Negotiating Skills

Personal details:

Date of birth: 1 October 1979
Interests: Swimming, golf
Member of West Sussex Choral Society
Voluntary trainer with the Southey Youth Association

Car owner/driver with full, clean UK licence
References available on request

Ellen Ashe
91 Stuart Close, Reach
Gloucester GL4 7XS
Tel: home: 0000 000000 mobile: 0000 000000

Career profile

Experienced personnel manager with expertise in both human resources and industrial relations, and with general management skills including administration and project leadership as well as overall staff management.

Key strengths

Knowledge of psychometric testing: qualified in the use of psychometric and profiling tools and have since administered over 250 tests, leading to better staff functioning and a noticeable increase in retention.

Professional attitude: Fellow of the Institute of Personnel and Development; 12 years' experience in HR, promoted three times within the same company; continuing programme of self-development through specialist vocational training.

Executive-level recruitment: organised complete personnel function for Cotswolds Head Office; successfully recruited Financial Director and Assistant Director as well as other key management personnel.

Key achievements

- Developing comprehensive human resource policy, reducing staff turnover and increasing efficiency and productivity
- Negotiating Partnership Agreement between management and unions
- Achieving 85% staff compliance with 24-hour telephone banking service
- Introducing Quality Programme of personnel-led productivity initiatives
- Devising and delivering focused induction training course to 350 employees
- Fellow of the Institute of Personnel and Development
- Qualified in the use of psychometric testing and profiling tools

Career history

2001 to present
Cotswolds Financial Services Group
Employee Relations Manager
Managed overall personnel function for office and general staff

- Undertook:
  - Complete IR function
  - Specialist employment consultancy
  - Project management
  - Social club management
- Developed personnel policies and procedures for financial group
- Improved effectiveness of human resource development strategies
- Managed introduction of performance evaluation system
- Extended skills in all aspects of personnel management
- Developed comprehensive knowledge of employment law, performance management and discipline handling

Ellen Ashe (cont.)

1992 to 2001
Personnel Manager (Sales Staff)
Personnel Manager (Head Office Staff)
Organised complete personnel function for Head Office and Southern Region Staff

- Managed personnel function for field-based staff, locally based office and general staff
- Administered records, pay and contractual documents
- Promoted from assistant personnel officer in 1990

1988 to 1992
Personnel Administration Supervisor
Responsible for administration of:

- records
- information
- pay
- contractual documents

1984 to 1988
Personnel Assistant

- Administrative and semi-technical support

1978 to 1984
Various
Clerical Assistant and Officer

- Personnel administration including recruitment, salaries, expenses, cash accounting
- Routine tax returns and administrative duties

Education and training

Work-related training:

- Psychometric testing
- Assessment skills
- Management training courses

Fardean College
1982 to 1984

- A levels: British Government, Economics

Episcopal Secondary School
1972 to 1978
GCSEs:

- Six including Maths, Economics and English

Professional

Fellow of the Institute of Personnel and Development

Personal

Date of birth:	17 October 1961
Health:	Non-smoker
Licence:	Full, clean UK driving licence
Interests:	Table tennis, including running local club Photography, City & Guilds qualified Swimming; music; voluntary work

Lee Daniels
42 Cartwright Crescent, St George
Bedford BD12 7GM
Tel: Home: 0000 0000000 Work: 0000 0000000
e-mail: ldaniels@easternaero.co.uk

Career profile

A challenging senior management position with a progressive company sought by an experienced Engineering Production Manager with 10 years' management experience, a strong background in aeronautical engineering and a high degree of technical as well as managerial skill.

Key strengths

Change manager with strong leadership skills: successfully administered closure of Eastern Aero-Engines London repair facility and transfer to Dublin with minimum disruption — plant fully operational within two weeks. Devised, negotiated and introduced new working practices to facilitate a steady 7–10 per cent annual growth in a more commercial environment.

Understanding of the aeronautical industry: extensive knowledge and experience gleaned during a career in the industry from project management and systems design through to production management. Member of the team responsible for bringing B77 engine from development into production.

Key skills

- Professional management skills
  - Meeting objectives
  - Identifying problems
  - Promoting solutions
  - Managing change
  - Setting and monitoring policy
  - Motivating and developing staff
- Extensive experience of aero-engine overhaul and repair management
- Knowledge of business systems with contracts experience
- Well-developed and effective communication skills

Career history

2005–present
Eastern Aero-Engines plc
Engine Overhaul Manager
Responsible for developing a sustainable and profitable Sea-horse repair business on engines, components and associated services:

- Achieved planned margins and cash flow
- Developed market opportunities and expanded business
- Negotiated contracts
- Interfaced with customers
- Allocated and managed resources to fulfil target commitments

Also administered closure of East London Repair Facility and transfer to Dublin.

Lee Daniels (cont.)

1998–2005

Repair Control Manager

Responsible for administration during contractual changes from Cost Plus to Fixed Price:

- Introduced new working practices to suit commercial environment
- Supervised contract administration
- Co-ordinated technical control and facility planning
- Maintained customer interface

Engines worked: Sea-horse, SD222 and Blair conversions.

1996–1998

Production Control Manager

Responsible for scheduling and logistic support of engine/module build programmes. Developed mechanical scheduling/monitoring and reporting system.

1992–1996

Inventory Manager

Responsible for order administration and inventory management for new engine projects. Planned and commissioned new Finished Parts Store (£1m project).

1985–1992

Systems Designer

Responsible for SDA system. Trialled SDA packages. Designed order entry systems.

1983–1985

Project Manager

Responsible for bringing B77 engine from development into production.

1980–1983

Section Leader

Qualifications

MIEE
HND Production Engineering
A levels: Maths, Physics

Work-related training:
Financial Management
Appraisal Techniques
Quality Control

Personal details

Date of birth:	1 June 1961
Licence:	Full, clean UK driving licence
Interests:	Sailing Hill-walking
References:	Available on request

Mistakes and makeovers

When you've completed your CV, take a little time to fine-tune it and give it a final polish. In this chapter we'll look at the things you must do, things you mustn't do, and how to turn a lacklustre CV into an interview-getting one.

Common mistakes

Here are some of the classic mistakes that crop up all too frequently in CVs. Check your own CV to make sure you have avoided these common pitfalls.

Spelling errors

A worryingly high number of recruiters say they would automatically discard any CV with spelling or grammar mistakes, yet time after time this is the commonest fault found in CVs. Spell-checkers are useful but they can't tell the difference between 'there' and 'their', for example, so get someone with a fresh eye to look over your CV before you send it.

Irrelevancy

You must demonstrate you have the desired competencies. These days, you have to tailor your CV to the job you're applying for – a general, one-size-fits-all approach won't help you to stand out against the competition. Make sure your CV addresses the employer's stated needs clearly and succinctly.

Making the reader search for information

The most important information – the knowledge, skills and experience that make you suitable for the job – goes on the first page of your CV in its own section so that the reader cannot miss it.

Messy layout

A messy layout makes your CV difficult to read and the information in it difficult to find. Opt for a clean, clear layout that groups information logically in easily digested chunks and lets the eye flow down the page – the simpler the better.

Waffling on

When people don't see relevant information, their attention can begin to wander after as little as 40 words. Be selective; stick to the key points and refine each sentence in your CV to make it as succinct as possible. If your CV runs to more than two A4 pages, edit it. Avoid any vague catch-all phrases and make sure every word counts.

Unsubstantiated claims

Everyone is a success-orientated, highly motivated team player with excellent communication skills – at least, according to their CV. You need to back up your claims if you're going to stand out. If these skills are important to the job you're applying for, highlight them and give examples of when, where and how well you've used them. Don't exaggerate and claim skills and competencies you don't have, either; it will quickly become obvious – if not on your CV, then at the interview.

The attention-getting CV

Having looked at the negatives you need to avoid, let's run through a checklist of the positives you should actively pursue:

Section: Career profile

Have you worded your career profile so that it reflects the company you are applying to and the job you are applying for?

Section: Key strengths

Do your chosen key strengths match those required by the company? Have you included actual examples to back up your statements? Have you included the most important things they should know about you?

Section: Key skills/achievements/experience/qualifications

Have you chosen key qualities that will be important in the job you are applying for?

Section: Career history

Have you fitted your experience to the job requirements? Have you included duties and responsibilities relevant to your application? Have you also included your achievements together with specific facts and figures where appropriate?

Section: Education and training

Have you included all your relevant training – academic *and* vocational?

CV hints and tips

- Do your homework before you apply. Find out about the company and the position, and tailor your Career profile and Key strengths section accordingly. Make sure your career history section is as relevant as possible.
- Concentrate on the specific requirements asked for and highlight the skills and qualities that meet their needs.
- Always include examples to support your claims.
- Write with a positive attitude: include your achievements, not just your duties and responsibilities.
- Be specific wherever possible: 'introduced a sales training programme that achieved a 23% increase in turnover'.
- Don't worry about blowing your own trumpet where justified. You are marketing yourself, so your CV needs to present your best qualities and most relevant skills and competencies.
- Make sure there are no grammar or spelling mistakes in the CV or covering letter.
- Keep your CV short and to the point with a clear, concise and logical format that's easy to read and follow.
- Send it with a carefully tailored covering letter emphasising the key aspects of your skills background that are a good match with the job requirements.

CV makeover

Compare the 'before' version of this CV with the 'after' one to see how information can be strengthened and highlighted to give a CV that:

- states all your relevant skills and qualities clearly;
- attracts interest;
- makes a good impression.

Before

CURICULUM VITAE

SURNAME: **PERRIS**
FORENAMES: **JOY HELEN MARY** (FEMALE)
AGE: **30**
DATE OF BIRTH: **12/5/79**
NATIONALITY: BRITISH
DEPENDENTS: 2 CHILDREN; AGES: 8; 5
MARITAL STATUS: SEPARATED PENDING DIVORCE
ADDRESS: 27 KINGSCOTE PLACE, LIMPNEY, SURREY SR1 2AA
TELEPHONE: 00000 000000

EDUCATION
September 1984 - July 1990
Porton Infants and Junior School

September 1990 - July 1995
Porton Comprehensive: obtained GCSE passes in English Language, English Literature, Needlework, Biology, History, Maths

October 1998 - June 2000
South London College: German GCSE (Evening Class); Pass

September 2007 - Present
Limpney Training Centre: CLAIT and Clerical/Supervisory Skills Course

EMPLOYMENT HISTORY
2004–2008 – Mutual Assurance Association
General Office Supervisor
Responsible for collation and administration of documents and records; the organisation of data within the department; dealing with queries to the department.

1997–2004 – Clipper Retail
Shop Assistant, rising to Duty Manager
Supervised staff and attended to customers in busy city-centre store. Responsible for daily administration of section including stock control, cashing up, section turnover and customer complaints.

1995–1997 – Danube Imports Ltd
Clerical Assistant

HOBBIES AND INTERESTS
I enjoy music, dancing and aerobics, and was a keen member of the parent governors' committee.

After

Joy decided to reply to the following job ad and revised her CV accordingly.

Owing to expansion, an Administration Supervisor vacancy has arisen in our Data Management department. The successful candidate will be responsible for two Data Support staff and directly involved in maintaining, updating and creating data files, ensuring that our clients get the best service possible, as well as all other aspects of administration. Accuracy and attention to detail are crucial, and applicants must possess good communication skills with the ability to work under pressure during peak periods. Excellent IT skills in general and knowledge of Word and Excel in particular are essential. Experience of high-volume data handling preferred, but full training will be given.

JOY PERRIS
27 Kingscote Place
Limpney, Surrey SR1 2AA

Tel: 00000 000000

Career profile

Office Supervisor with four years' experience of organising data and records, and the tried and tested ability to maintain a consistently high standard of work and attention to detail under pressure and to motivate staff to do the same. Now looking for a challenging work environment where recently updated and enhanced computer skills can be put to good use ensuring the efficient working of a busy and demanding department.

Key strengths

Excellent IT skills: recently completed an advanced CLAIT course with a mark of 94%, having used computer skills extensively in a position of office supervisor.

Supervisory skills: successfully completed NVQ level 3 in Administration and Supervision and have been responsible for staff both as an office supervisor and as a retail duty manager.

Accuracy and attention to detail: retrieved and administered a high volume of documents and records for a busy insurance company to the highest degree of satisfaction of the Department Manager.

Client focused: used to dealing with sometimes complex interdepartmental queries courteously and efficiently as well as having been trained in customer focus in a retail environment.

Key skills

- Supervising staff
- Implementing procedures accurately
- Prioritising workload
- Computer skills – Microsoft Office:
  Word
  Excel
  PowerPoint
  Outlook

Career history

2007– present: Limpney Training Centre
CLAIT advanced course to update and extend IT and office management skills
NVQ level 3 Clerical Skills Course; Administration and Supervision

2004–present: Mutual Assurance Association
Office Supervisor
Responsible for collation and administration of documents and records; the organisation of data within the department; and dealing with queries to the department.

- Successfully trained a total of four administrative assistants
- Developed new procedures as the department grew, maintaining the highest standards of efficiency and accuracy
- Reorganised the query process to provide a more user-friendly format
- Established comprehensive basic procedures manual for staff training purposes

1997–2004: Clipper Retail Stores
Duty Manager
Supervised a total of seven staff and attended to customers in busy city-centre store. Responsible for daily administration of section including stock control, cashing up, section turnover and customer complaints.

- Maintained store within top 5% turnover
- Reduced shoplifting and petty pilfering by 20% by slightly altering section layout
- Reviewed sales training with regard to administering the Lottery, leading to a substantial reduction in customer complaints
- Promoted from Retail Assistant in 2000

1995–1997: Danube Imports Ltd
Clerical Assistant
Dealt with office administration including bookkeeping and invoicing.

Education
Porton Comprehensive – 6 GCSE passes, including English and Maths
South London College – GCSE pass in German
Limpney Training Centre – CLAIT and NVQ3 Clerical, Administration and Supervisory Skills

Personal details
Date of birth – 12 May 1979
Health – Non-smoker
Driving – Full, clean UK licence
Proficient German speaker
Interests – Music, dancing, aerobics. Served as a Parent Governor on primary school Governing Body; involved in decisions on budgets, curriculum and other management issues.

Although it's a little longer, the revised CV still only runs to two pages and manages to put the most relevant information about job skills and career history on the first page, leaving the less important facts about education and personal details for the second page.

Note that the revised CV:

- is much easier to read;
- looks much more professional;
- gives much more information;
- is specifically tailored to the job being applied for;
- gives more relevant information – things an employer will want to know;
- clearly highlights skills and experience;
- includes achievements;
- puts key competencies and relevant skills in at-a-glance sections that are hard to miss.

Let's look at another successful makeover. This time it's the CV of a school leaver who didn't think she had very much to offer.

Before

Pamela Heart
87 First Road
Impney
Hereford HE15 6TD

Tel: 00000 000000
e-mail: coolprincess@partyparty.co.uk

Education
2001–2008 Heath House King's School
GCSEs:
French B
History C

Maths C
General Science C
English Language D

A levels:
French C
History C

Work experience
2008 – Volunteer sheltered housing aid visitor
2007 and 2008 – Volunteer coach for holiday play scheme

Interests
Tennis and badminton
Athletics
Socialising and meeting new people

Date of birth: 20 April 1990

A very sparse CV with little for an employer to get their teeth into. But even this CV can be improved. This is the job ad that Pamela replied to:

Customer Care Team
Hours: Monday to Friday 0900–1700

Salary: £________________ pa

Working in our Customer Enquiries Office, you will be computer literate and have good communication skills. An articulate, friendly, helpful manner would be an advantage.

This position would suit a school leaver. Full training will be given, and there are many opportunities for advancement within the company.

Please contact ________________________________.

Pamela knew she had the skills and personal qualities needed to do the job and customised her CV so that the employer knew it.

After

Pamela Heart
87 First Road, Impney
Hereford HE15 6TD

Tel: 0000 000000
e-mail: psheart@anyisp.co.uk

Personal profile
A friendly, outgoing person. Reliable, conscientious and happy to work both as part of a team and on own initiative.

Key strengths
Good communication skills and a helpful manner: voluntary work with both elderly people and younger children has developed a good range of communication skills as well as the ability to help and support others conscientiously and diplomatically.

IT skills: full PC literacy including spreadsheets, e-mail, the internet and word processing

Achievements
- Represented the school in Athletics and Cross-Country Running
- Participated in City Marathon 2008
- Secretary of Under-18 Squash and Racquet team
- Elected House Captain

Education
2001–2008 Heath House King's School
A levels:
French C; History C
Computer skills
Microsoft XP including:
- Word
- Access
- Excel

GCSEs:
French B; History C; Maths C; General Science C; English Language D

Work experience
Working with elderly people: regularly visited four residents of local sheltered housing to help with shopping and everyday household tasks.

Holiday play scheme: coached under-11s in squash, badminton and tennis in groups of four or five during summer and Easter holidays.

Personal details
Date of birth: 20 April 1990
Non-smoker

Pamela's new CV is not only more informative generally but also tells the employer exactly what they want to know. Note the change of e-mail address, by the way.

Appendix: Words and phrases

Finding the right word is often one of the hardest parts of writing a CV. This appendix has examples of positive words and phrases for you to use, which might remind you of skills and qualities you want to include, and also help you to expand on those keywords. It contains:

- positive characteristics;
- action words;
- positive descriptions;
- benefits and achievements;
- desirable qualities.

Positive characteristics

These words describe personal attributes that are often seen as positive and useful in the workplace. Choose the words that describe you best:

Able	Adroit	Ambitious
Accurate	Adventurous	Analytical
Adaptable	Alert	Appreciative

Articulate
Assertive
Astute
Attractive

Bilingual
Bright

Calm
Capable
Competent
Confident
Consistent
Co-operative
Creative

Decisive
Dedicated
Dependable
Diligent
Diplomatic
Dynamic

Educated
Effective
Efficient
Energetic
Enthusiastic
Experienced
Expert

Fast
Firm
Fit
Flexible
Friendly

Gregarious

Hardworking
Healthy
Honest
Human
Humane

Imaginative
Independent
Informed
Ingenious
Innovative
Intelligent
Inventive

Knowledgeable

Literate
Loyal

Mature
Methodical
Motivated
Multilingual

Non-smoking

Objective
Open-minded
Organised
Outgoing
Outstanding

Patient
People-oriented
Perceptive
Persistent
Personable
Pioneering
Poised
Practical
Principled
Productive
Professional
Proficient
Punctual

Qualified
Quick
Quick-thinking

Rational
Ready
Realistic
Reliable
Resourceful
Responsible
Robust

Scrupulous
Self-assured
Self-confident
Self-motivated
Self-reliant
Sensitive
Serious
Shrewd
Skilled
Smart
Spirited
Stable

Strong	Thorough	Well-educated
Successful	Thoughtful	Well-groomed
Supportive	Trained	Willing
	Trustworthy	Witty
Tactful		
Talented	Versatile	Young
Tenacious	Vigorous	Youthful

Action words

These are positive, active words that you can use to describe your responsibilities and achievements.

(All the words here are in the past tense – they all end in 'ed' – which is right for the Career history section of your CV. If you want to use them in the Key skills section, change the 'ed' to 'ing' to turn it into the present tense; for example:
Key skills: Organising meetings and functions, purchasing stationery
Career history: Organised meetings and functions, purchased stationery)

Accelerated	Booked	Contributed
Accessed	Broadened	Controlled
Achieved	Budgeted	Co-ordinated
Acquired		Correlated
Acted	Checked	Created
Administered	Coached	
Advised	Collaborated	Delegated
Analysed	Competed	Demonstrated
Appointed	Completed	Designed
Appraised	Communicated	Determined
Arranged	Compiled	Developed
Assigned	Conceived	Devised
Assisted	Conducted	Diagnosed
Attended	Consulted	Directed

Doubled

Edited
Effected
Eliminated
Enabled
Established
Evaluated
Executed
Exercised
Expanded
Expedited
Explored

Facilitated
Fostered
Formulated
Founded

Generated
Guided

Handled
Harmonised
Headed
Helped
Hired

Identified
Implemented
Improved
Increased
Initiated
Installed
Instituted
Instructed
Interacted
Invented
Investigated

Launched
Led
Liaised

Maintained
Managed
Marketed
Mentored
Monitored
Motivated

Negotiated

Opened
Operated
Organised
Oversaw

Participated
Performed
Pinpointed
Pioneered
Planned
Prepared
Presented
Processed
Produced
Programmed
Promoted
Proposed
Provided
Purchased

Recommended
Recruited
Recorded
Reduced
Reorganised
Reported
Represented
Researched
Resolved
Restored
Restructured
Reviewed
Revised

Saved
Scheduled
Secured
Selected
Set up
Shaped
Sold
Solved
Structured
Supervised

Taught
Tested
Trained

Upgraded
Used
Utilised

Visualised

Won
Wrote

Positive descriptions

As well as using positive words for your characteristics and achievements, there are also a variety of ways to describe your strengths.

Instead of saying 'I am good at. . .', you could say:

I am skilled at. . .
I am a skilful. . .
I possess a degree of ability in. . .
I am very good at. . .
I am extremely good at. . .
I am exceptional at. . .
I am adept at. . .
I am an expert in. . .
I excel at. . .
I have the ability to. . .
I am competent in. . .
I am an experienced. . .
I am a deft. . .
I have a talent for. . .
I am familiar with. . .
I am qualified to. . .

For example:

- I am skilled at facilitating the exchange of ideas
- I am a skilful communicator
- I have a high degree of ability in computer programming
- I am adept at promoting policy changes
- I am very good at handling a variety of tasks efficiently
- I am exceptional at motivating large or small groups
- I have a talent for budget projection

- I am familiar with a wide range of software
- I am qualified to assess retail training up to NVQ level 3

Benefits

Employers want to feel confident that the person they employ will take problems off their hands. They are looking for people who can do any of the following:

Increase	Decrease	Improve
Profits	Staff turnover	Competitive advantage
Product turnover	Risks	Appearance and/or marketability
Sales	Time taken	Organisation
Efficiency	Potential problems	Information flow
Market opportunities	Costs	Staff performance
	Waste	Teamwork and relationships

Make sure your CV includes any of the above benefits that you have achieved in your job.

Desirable qualities

The following characteristics are rated the most desirable by the majority of employers. Although many of them seem quite obvious, they are the sort of things that can easily be forgotten when thinking about your qualities and characteristics. Bear them in mind when compiling your CV and include them, where relevant and appropriate, in your personal profile or career profile.

Employers prefer someone who is:
Reliable
Punctual
Trustworthy
Friendly
Willing to learn
Enthusiastic
Accurate
Able to work as part of a team
Able to follow instructions accurately
Able to handle problems, and refer them on, appropriately
Able to work with colleagues, customers or clients.

Employers look for someone who:
Has a positive attitude
Takes pride in their work
Has a suitable appearance
Has initiative.

Putting it together

Use the 'template' CV on the next page as a guide to where you might find suitable words and phrases for each particular section.

Play around with the words in this appendix and the examples in Chapter 2 until you arrive at something that describes both you and the work you have done, accurately and positively.

Don't forget to mine the job ad or job description for ideas. Read several ads for the sort of job you intend to apply for to give you a feel for the sort of descriptive words that are used in your particular field. You can include those that apply to you in your CV. See Chapters 2 and 3 for more on this topic, and look at Chapter 4 for advice about keywords.

Career profile

(Look at **Keywords, Positive characteristics, Positive descriptions** and **Desirable qualities**)

Key strengths

(Look at **Keywords, Positive descriptions, Benefits, Desirable qualities and Action words**)

Key skills

(Look at **Keywords, Positive descriptions** and **Action words**)

-
-
-

Career history

(Name of company)

(Dates you worked there)

(Job title)

(Job responsibilities. Look at **Keywords** and **Action words**)

- (Achievements and responsibilities. Look at **Keywords, Action words**
- and **Benefits**)
-
-

(Name of company)

(Dates you worked there)

(Job title)

(Job responsibilities. Look at **Keywords** and **Action words**)

- (Achievements and responsibilities. Look at **Keywords, Action words**
- and **Benefits**)
-
-